Dear Seamus,

MERRY CHRISTMAS!

lots of love,

Marie

(AKA - THE-ONE-WHO-JUST-WON'T-LEAVE-HOME...)

Full Irish

Full Irish
New Architecture in Ireland

Sarah A. Lappin

Princeton Architectural Press, New York

Published by
Princeton Architectural Press
37 East Seventh Street
New York, New York 10003

For a free catalog of books, call 1.800.722.6657.
Visit our website at www.papress.com.

Photo credits:
Front cover: Mimetic House by Dominic Stevens Architect,
photo by Ros Kavanagh
Back cover: Solstice Centre by Grafton Architects,
photo by Ros Kavanagh
5 bottom, 6, 11: Sarah A. Lappin
ii, vi, 5 top, 12–13: Andy Frew

Project editor: Clare Jacobson
Copy editor: Dan Fernandez
Designer: Jan Haux

Special thanks to: Nettie Aljian, Bree Anne Apperley, Sara Bader,
Nicola Bednarek, Janet Behning, Becca Casbon, Carina Cha,
Penny (Yuen Pik) Chu, Carolyn Deuschle, Russell Fernandez,
Pete Fitzpatrick, Wendy Fuller, Aileen Kwun, Nancy Eklund Later,
Linda Lee, Laurie Manfra, John Myers, Katharine Myers,
Lauren Nelson Packard, Dan Simon, Andrew Stepanian,
Jennifer Thompson, Paul Wagner, Joseph Weston, and Deb Wood
of Princeton Architectural Press —Kevin C. Lippert, publisher

Library of Congress Cataloging-in-Publication Data
Lappin, Sarah A. (Sarah Anne), 1972–
Full Irish : new architecture in Ireland / Sarah A. Lappin.
p. cm.
Includes bibliographical references.
ISBN 978-1-56898-868-9 (alk. paper)
1. Architecture—Ireland—History—20th century. 2. Architecture—
Ireland—History—21st century. 3. Architecture—Northern Ireland—
History—20th century. 4. Architecture—Northern Ireland—History—
21st century. I. Title.
NA989.L37 2009
720.9415'0904—dc22
                                                          2008050460

Table of Contents

Introduction
Fully Irish: Identity and Context

The New York World's Fair in 1939 brought to a public readying for war such well-documented events as Alvar Aalto's jaw-dropping Finnish pavilion and Oscar Niemeyer and Lúcio Costa's collaboration for the Brazilian entry. Few people know it was the Irish pavilion, designed by Irish architect William Scott, that was chosen by a jury of international judges as the best building in the show. To represent a nation that was at the time a mere seventeen years old, Scott was instructed to design a building in the then avant-garde style of high modernism yet still recognizably "Irish." His pavilion was to show the world that Ireland was a society on the cutting edge, free of its former colonial rulers, willing and able to emulate fashionable architecture from outside its borders, while still appealing to the millions of Irish Americans who would see the show and its printed materials. So Scott employed what one would expect from the modernist vocabulary: white walls, soaring glazed window walls, and visible circulation in concrete and steel. All he needed was the Irish bit, and he decided to insert that in the building's plan.

The pavilion was built in the shape of a shamrock.

Purpose and Practice

This book is an introduction to contemporary Irish architecture for those unfamiliar with its built form and its geographic, political, social, and cultural context. It examines the work of sixteen firms from the Republic of Ireland as well as Northern Ireland from various generations. As much as possible, the work shown here is built on the island of Ireland, and all of the firms have their main offices there as well.

Good architecture in the Republic and Northern Ireland is not limited to the work shown in this volume, of course. However, as the built environment of Ireland, both North and South, now undergoes more rapid changes than at any other time in history, it is not enough, for this author, that architects design good or even great buildings. Architects must engage in dialogue with planners, developers, clients, educators, and, most importantly, users to ensure excellence in architectural design and the built environment in this era of rapid change. *Full Irish: New Architecture in Ireland* thus highlights these practices as much for their design abilities as for their engagement in architectural debate and the continued wide dissemination of an architectural culture. They are in discussion, at a variety of levels, about the future of architecture on the island; they teach, write, debate, and constantly question their responses to conditions. These firms interrogate not only sites but briefs, well-entrenched typologies, and, as discussed later, the more difficult questions of identity within globalization.

The book is constructed around two or three conversations with every firm, each ranging over a number of hours, discussing its own work, the current environment in Ireland for building, influences, goals, styles of working, and defining moments. These conversations took place over two years, in model-filled offices, on construction sites, in completed buildings, via email and, to enjoy the cliché as much as possible, in pubs.[1] Most of the travel for the book was on public transportation and, particularly in Dublin, on foot; this perspective on the climate of development is evident throughout the text.

In addition to profiles of eleven firms with three to four projects each, *Full Irish* includes five sections on smaller practices. In some cases, these are young firms, in the nascence of their roles as independent designers, still discovering their priorities and voices. In other cases, the firms are headed by architects for whom written or taught research makes up a significant part of their practice. For them, making architecture is more

heavily influenced by in-depth thinking and writing rather than in achieving final built forms for specific clients on actual sites. If this book were to be written ten, five, even three years from now, any of these firms may have expanded into larger projects; certainly they all have the capacity do to so.

Adaptation of Imports

Issues of Irish architectural identity can be traced much farther back than 1939. Architectural historians identify Roman influences in early Irish churches as early as A.D. 600. Round towers have been likened to similar structures in Italy. Elements of the so-called Irish Romanesque can be traced to Rhenish, English, German, Swiss, and French sources. After 1700, the organizational patterns for most Irish towns and cities were concretized, heavily seasoned with neoclassical buildings and layouts. At this time, the most popular style for importation was the Palladian. The principles of John Ruskin, too, were introduced, particularly by architects Sir Thomas Deane and Benjamin Woodward.

The tradition of Ireland as a petri dish for architecture continued into the twentieth century, unsurprisingly, given the effect of early mass media on architects. The influence of the International Style can be seen in the main Dublin Airport terminal, built in 1940 by Desmond Fitzgerald for the Office of Public Works, and in Michael Scott's Busáras bus terminal in Dublin. Robin Walker, of Scott Tallon Walker, returned to Ireland with his lessons learned in Chicago with Mies van der Rohe. STW's Carroll's tobacco factory in Dundalk represents the pinnacle of this Hiberno-Miesian style, and John Meagher, of de Blacam and Meagher Architects, proclaims that it was this firm that "taught us [current practitioners] how to build." Sean O'Laoire goes so far as to say that Ireland is "a product of its roles as a proto-colonial laboratory."[2] Architectural styles were never imported unaltered, however, and the label of "distinctly Irish" is applied early in architectural history. This flavor is "characterized by simplicity, and spareness, informality, and not a little fantasy."[3] That most Irish interpretations of European models seem simpler, more pared down, has been ascribed variously to a weaker economy and a lack of skilled artisans. Many point to the Georgian Dublin terraces as the most potent example of this—they entail large proportions and grand spaces as per their European relatives of the time, but with little extraneous decoration or adornment. Much has been made of the connection between Irish and Swiss architecture in recent years. Niall McCullough of McCullough Mulvin Architects notes, however, that there is a fundamental "difference between deciding to state things simply [as in Swiss examples] and having to" because of economic constraints, as in Irish architecture.

With a history perceived as important, can this or any other volume about architecture from this island ever refer to an "Irish" architecture? Perhaps the better question is this: is a single architectural identity important or indeed necessary in the early twenty-first century?

Fully Irish?

This question fuels a debate between both Irish architects and those who observe them from outside. Before the Irish economy began its "miraculous" recovery in the late 1980s, a generation of architects, including O'Donnell + Tuomey, Grafton, and McCullough Mulvin spent time inwardly examining the then existing built environment of the country. It is not insignificant that much of this introspection occurred simultaneously with postulations of critical regionalism propounded by Alexander Tzonis, Liane Lefaivre, and Kenneth Frampton.

Contemporary Irish architects can't seem to agree on a single narrative. O'Donnell + Tuomey feel that though "we are definitely Irish architects, we discovered our

work through working here," their approach has "wider applications to other settings abroad." Grafton doesn't set out to impart an "Irishness" but to concentrate on the cultural climate in which it currently sits. Any Irishness that imbues its work happens by virtue of working in this particular place; it is not something pursued for its own sake.

Boyd Cody would argue that "part of being Irish is about being open to other influences." Shih-Fu Peng of heneghan.peng.architects goes farther and states that he has not seen an emergent Irish style. Peng came to Ireland from the United States in 2000, and for him, the specificity of place has much to do with the scale, speed, and politics at which one can work. "In Holland, concepts must be a minimum of 1:50, in Switzerland 1:2. In China, it's at 1:100 or even larger." During the economic boom, building in Ireland meant the appropriate level of scale changed rapidly. Dublin's massive expansion, in particular, meant designing at the traditional medium scale had to be questioned.

FKL does not pursue an overtly Irish style, either. "We're architects first. Nationality is not a driving force. We all speak the same language, have similar referents." For FKL, Irishness in many ways can be distilled to what the local construction industry can do, and can do well. This reflects an attitude of architects working in Northern Ireland—for Alan Jones and Hackett Hall McKnight, the local construction industry plays a large part in the nature of building in this region. For these northern firms, this characteristic is specific to the region and must be treated as a key component of any architecture made there.

In many ways, the most intriguing firm in Ireland from this perspective is MacGabhann Architects of Donegal, in the island's northwesternmost region. The two brothers took over their father's practice, and both have Irish as their first language. They are fluent in local history and culture, literature, and folklore. However, their experience working in other parts of Europe imbues their architecture with a decidedly different formal language than that found in the surrounding landscape. They employ materials in a manner not seen in this quiet part of the island; their buildings insist that users engage with the landscape of Donegal through visual and physical connections. This firm is committed to "being Irish" in cultural terms while still using influences from outside the region.

Some of the architecture in this volume is not without its critics. Aaron Betsky argues that Irish architecture borrows too heavily from traditions that may not be entirely relevant in place and time. He hopes that this consensus of design, though borrowed, "could be taught to a next generation of architects so that they can adopt and adapt it into a more coherent and native idiom."[4] For him, it is of utmost importance that the architects working in Ireland develop "an authentic language of architecture, tied to history and material."[5]

Jean-Louis Cohen, on the other hand, insists that Irish architects "have achieved a particular identity through their own means."[6] Writing in 2001 in the midst of economic prosperity, he saw a tension between the booming Irish economy and the aspirations of architects who espoused critical regionalism in the late eighties and early nineties. He calls the approach of contemporary Irish architects "critical internationalism." This approach allows for "research for a local specificity" while not precluding "a series of cross positions defining a common intellectual space."[7] The increasingly international character of capital, clients, and uses in Ireland allows—perhaps forces—a direct connection to architectures happening throughout the world and in Europe especially.

For American-born Merritt Bucholz of Bucholz McEvoy, whether this architecture can be expressive of "an Irishness" is an issue of what he calls an "unfinished symphony." The buildings and spaces being created now need time to be measured for their impact on the society in which they sit. "Because we've had fifteen years of boom, we haven't yet had a time of maturing, a period of calm to absorb what this new society and architecture in it mean." Now that the economic condition has decelerated considerably, architects and clients alike may have this time for reflection.

Perhaps the inability to establish a codified, unified notion of an Irish architectural identity persists in its difficulty because of this age-old tension—the long history of architectural imports being adapted by local building skills, materials, climate, and now by an ever-more heterogeneous society. As Irish culture becomes increasingly multifaceted, with disparate backgrounds of those who commission, make, and, perhaps most importantly, inhabit architecture, the nature of a fully Irish architecture is one that must be continuously questioned. This is a globalized island in architectural terms, and has been for centuries, but this is the first time in which cultural norms have changed so rapidly largely because of a phenomenon seemingly unthinkable twenty years ago: immigration. The critical regionalism that many would have as the predominant force must be tempered by a discussion of the reality of the changing nature of society on the island of Ireland. One can argue that Ireland, including the North, though perhaps more slowly, has undergone more social, economic, and cultural change in the last fifteen years than at any previous period in its history. Architecture should be considered not simply as a "fit" to the formal or material context but also in the way these spaces will now be used and how they will symbolize a new Irish society.

Shifts in Acceptance

Since the 1970s, there has been a slow but growing interest in contemporary architecture on the island of Ireland, particularly in the Republic. For many, the single most important event that changed attitudes toward contemporary architecture in the Republic was the competition held in 1991 by Dublin City Council to revitalize the Temple Bar area of the city center. Until 1990 the city had planned to create a gargantuan bus station in an area of existing narrow streets and three- and four-story, high-density buildings. Because the area had been blighted with the undesirability that festered in many inner-city areas, rents were low, and an informal community of artists, musicians, and writers had established itself there. As the city began a slow regeneration in the late 1980s, an increased desire for city-center apartments made urban living more attractive; locals began to take issue with the proposed demolition of the Temple Bar area's traditional street layout and scale of fabric.

The competition was awarded to a consortium of eight small young firms called Group 91. Their overall plan was not "one single solution, rather a flexible series of integrated responses."[8] For them, this was a plan for three thousand "citizens," individuals living and working in a modern democracy. Their designs called for a few new streets, for two new public squares within the urban framework, and for individual buildings, mainly based around cultural projects and living spaces for those working in the area.

It was the first time that contemporary architecture by young architects had been built on such a large scale and in such a concentrated area. Here were numerous public and private buildings as well as new spaces carved from the existing fabric that did not speak in a language of pastiche. It was a first, too, for using cultural programs to give the impetus for an inner-city project.

Though the area has since become less a cultural heart for the city and instead a den of tourists and bachelor party revelers, it can be argued that this single project influenced the loosening of conservative planners and clients more than any other single factor. The acceptance, even demand, for contemporary architecture since 1991 owes much to the competition and its skilled winners.

Beauty...

A common theme for many of the practices discussed in the sections that follow is an absorption in the landscape, both built and unbuilt. Much has been written about the beauty of Ireland, and an effort to re-create the work of centuries of artists, musicians, and poets will not be attempted here. However, to put it simply, to understand the Irish landscape is to comprehend battered coastline, rolling farmland, bleak hillsides, and the light and water that continuously affect a reading of them. The coast is inhabited by both small village ports and large industrial sites like Cork, Belfast, and Dublin. Donegal has numerous small uninhabited beaches, while cliffs dominate much of the west and northeast coasts. Much of the interior of Ireland is the typical rolling green hills one sees in postcards, but these give over quickly to flat farmland, high moors, and peat bog lands. In the west is the Burren, an ancient moonscape of an area covered in fissured limestone pavement and not much else.

People who come to Ireland for the first time are of course struck by its million shades of green but also by the quality of the light. In summer, daylight can be celebrated from as early as 4:00 a.m. and used until 11:00 p.m., while in winter, one can rely on good light only from 9:00 a.m. until about 3:00 p.m. The fact that Ireland is so far north plays a part in this quality, as do the common low-pressure systems that dilute the light into haze, a shadowless gray that pervades the landscape for days at a time. Light, except on rare days of either blazing sunshine or absolute soul-numbing gray, is ever changing in Ireland—flighty one minute, pouring in through every available crack in the next.

The landscape in Ireland is permeated by water, whether through its proximity to the coastline or to lakes, rivers, bogs, and marshlands. And it rains. A lot. For T. G. Mitchell, it is largely the "way precipitation moves through and over the ground . . . [that] determines the visual form of our environment."[9]

. . . and the Beast

In 2006, the Venice Biennale Irish Pavilion, curated by FKL Architects, posed the problem: how to cope with the ever-expanding sprawl that eats into the former hinterlands of Irish cities? Particularly in light of growing populations and decreasing household sizes, the management of the edge conditions concerns many architects and critics throughout the island. The notion of sustainable, high-density cities has not yet been embraced by the Irish public, for the most part. European models of this type of high-density housing are the usual referents for solutions to the problem; many of the architects in this volume attempt to find a resolution specific to the society and landscape of twenty-first-century Ireland.

Procurement of large public projects continues to provide serious anxiety for the profession, particularly in Northern Ireland. Architects are concerned that with the United Kingdom's governmental commitment to Private Finance Initiative, the designer's role is increasingly excluded from the provision of new buildings. With billions being pumped into Northern Ireland for capital projects, mainly schools and hospitals, any lack of considered design in schemes will have a serious, long-reaching impact on major public buildings and thus the larger built environment.

The development of rural communities also concerns many of the architects in this volume, MacGabhann and Dominic Stevens in particular. Both practices are located outside the major cities of Ireland—in Donegal and Leitrim, respectively. The huge increase in second homes populating the countryside has caused considerable debate in rural communities. In Northern Ireland, where legislation about rural development is, for the time being, far stricter than in the Republic, much is made of the development patterns just across the border in Donegal. Some point to the ability of new development to raise land prices and ensure prosperity for hard-hit farmers, while others argue that the sprawl decimates the landscape and burdens future generations with unsustainable communities.

Unlike areas in Scotland that have been cleared yet remain deserted, or regions of the American West that were never previously settled, the Irish rural landscape has been filled with people. Famine in the 1840s decimated the overall population by several million; houses and villages that had been scattered throughout the landscape fell into ruin and have been eaten by time and geology. To insist that the landscape remain deserted—to "leave the unspoilt nature alone"—would be historically inaccurate and fails to acknowledge the heavily human-made nature of the landscape in the first place. However, it is becoming increasingly apparent that a pattern of expansion that results in ribbon developments of large-scale homes standing empty for much of the year must be rigorously, and quickly, reconsidered. As an island heavily dependent on external energy sources, Ireland must aggressively interrogate the sustainability of its development immediately.

Life Abroad?

The earlier discussion of identities must also be read in light of a tradition for architectural life abroad. Architects from Ireland were forced, for generations, to look for work elsewhere, often in Europe and North America. In addition to the economic pressure this implied, the issue had a more significant problem for the development of critical practice at the time: in the 1970s and 1980s, Ireland had little overt, focused architectural culture. Sheila O'Donnell notes that when "we were at college, there was little recognition of an architectural culture in Ireland. We went away to immerse ourselves in the London scene that at that time was focused on rediscovering some sort of continuity with the culture of European architecture."

The list of alumni organizations is impressive. Some earned degrees at schools like Princeton, Harvard, and Columbia in the United States, while others went to schools in the United Kingdom, such as Cambridge and the Mackintosh School of Art, for the second part of their degrees. They include the offices of Emilio Ambasz, Wiel Arets, Alberto Campo Baeza, Michael Graves, Louis Kahn, Daniel Liebeskind, John Pawson, James Stirling, Venturi Scott Brown, Álvaro Siza Vieira, and other firms in cities like Berlin, Frankfurt, London, and Paris. For those who went abroad, the experience often not only gave them time to absorb architectural methodologies in the office of a "master" but also forced them to define themselves as people, designers, and thinkers.

With the boom in the economy of the Republic of Ireland since the 1990s, and with a recent wave of enormous government investment for capital projects in Northern Ireland, young students and new graduates did not need to emigrate in large numbers. The demand for their skills, however nascent, was considerable from firms of all sizes in both parts of the island. For many students from the North, "down South" was a significantly foreign enough place to train; a growing number of highly skilled and busy practices made staying at home a viable and attractive option. Some of the most exciting architecture in the world was being created by firms on the island of Ireland—why go abroad?

What will happen to Irish architecture if most young blood does not venture beyond the pale remains to be seen. Many of the more seasoned architects who were forced into the broader architectural world feel this will not only impinge on architectural ideas but also diminish young architects' understanding of other cultures, however similar or dissimilar. Though the great equalizer of world travel, the low-cost airline, has made frequent journeys to see great buildings possible, the diverse vocabulary of tectonic form and personal experience will see a shift from previous generations of Irish architects. However, at this writing, the clouds of recession bode ill for the construction industry in both the Republic and in Northern Ireland. A new wave of young architects may be bridging out again, though this time instead of German, Portuguese, or inner-city American, these travelers may have to learn to work in Arabic or Mandarin and live in countries much farther away.

A Woman's Place

One of the most startling aspects about firms in Ireland is the unusually high number of women practicing architecture. The American Institute of Architects lists 11 percent of its members as female. The Royal Institute of British Architects vacillates between 11 and 13 percent, depending on the year; this statistic includes Northern Ireland. The Royal Institute of the Architects of Ireland, though, counts 30 percent. Perhaps more striking is the number of firms headed by women and the fact that finding women in leading positions in Irish architecture takes no effort; many of them are illustrated here.

Why this is the case is difficult to answer and is an area for future research. When one looks to progenitors of Irish architecture generally, one must accord serious importance to Eileen Gray for her groundbreaking furniture designs, understanding of modernist space at her house E1027, and her treatment of interiors therein. Whatever the background reason, gender does not appear to be an issue for these architects—there seems to be little question of inequality, and the issue was never raised in conversations about context by any of the practitioners interviewed.

Conclusions

The mood of the architectural community in Ireland is reminiscent of typical Irish weather patterns—sunny, optimistic, worth buying sunglasses for one moment, and dour, dark, and miserable the next. Irish architects regularly win international awards and design competitions. On the one hand, a book like this is possible because of numerous projects of serious caliber, many of which represent a commitment on the part of government clients to allocate considerable budgets for significant projects. On the other, the monster of uncontrolled sprawl outside Ireland's major cities and into its rural landscapes has forced people to fall out of love with their country; mind-boggling traffic problems, poor construction, and lack of sustainable thinking decimate a sense of place.

Lázló Moholy-Nagy insisted that "one can never experience art through descriptions. Explanations and analysis can serve at best as intellectual preparation."[10] If you have any interest, no matter how small, in this architecture, your understanding must not be limited to its visual projection in these pages. You are not an "audience" of architecture—you inhabit, use, work in, delight in, are depressed in, and live in it. Surely architecture is about being *within*, not examining from *without*, about being an active user, not a passive audience member.

Go visit these buildings, where appropriate. Many of them are public institutions; this effort on the part of governments to produce extremely high-quality cultural buildings by architects engaged in an intellectually rigorous architecture should be appreciated and celebrated as much and by as many people as possible.

1 All unsourced quotes in this book are taken from personal interviews between the speaker and the author between March 2006 and December 2008.
2 Sean O'Laoire, "Building on the Edge of Europe," in *Building on the Edge of Europe*, ed. John Graby (Dublin: Royal Institute of the Architects of Ireland, 1996), 123.
3 Ibid, 20.
4 Aaron Betsky, "Dublin from a Bird's-Eye View," in *New Irish Architecture 19: AAI Awards 2004*, ed. Nicola Dearey and John O'Regan (Dublin: Gandon Editions, 2004), 9.
5 Ibid.
6 Jean-Louis Cohen, "Ireland's Critical Internationalism," in *New Irish Architecture 16: AAI Awards 2001*, ed. Nicola Dearey and John O'Regan (Dublin: Gandon Editions, 2001), 7.
7 Ibid., 8.
8 Group 91, "The Temple Bar Framework Plan: A Community of 3,000 Citizens Living in the City," in *Temple Bar Lives!* ed. Jobst Grave (Dublin: Temple Bar Properties, 1991), 16.
9 T. G. Mitchell, "Building and the Landscape," in Graby, *Building on the Edge of Europe*, 20.
10 Lázló Moholy-Nagy, quoted in Michael Trencher, *The Alvar Aalto Guide* (New York: Princeton Architectural Press, 1996), 23.

Alma Lane

Boyd Cody Architects

The architecture of Dermot Boyd and Peter Cody, which manifests itself in this volume in domestic settings, is in many ways difficult to grasp. The buildings, at first glance, appear to be stripped-down versions of the idea of "house," with minimal palettes and strong geometric moves. A passing examination of the formal gestures of their buildings certainly reveals the experience of Boyd at John Pawson's office in London. However, given the opportunity to explore these spaces in person or to examine in detail the drawings and images used in the design process, one realizes that Boyd Cody engage in a rigor of questioning and in a depth of detail rarely seen in architecture. The most minute moves—handrails, benches, thresholds—do not exist in any catalog, nor are they recycled from previous projects. Every element in their buildings, from roof detail to the type of covering for a sink unit, is an extraordinary materialization of months of thinking, specific to site, client, and use.

As one would expect of architects who interrogate every layer of their projects with such precision, they are also not content to leave any architectural typology untested. Boyd Cody would as soon choose an off-the-shelf solution to the design of space as they would a window detail from a manufacturer's stock list. Rather, they inquire how the spaces are to be used—yes, it should answer the fundamental requirements of "living," but is there a response embedded in the site as well? Here one catches a glimpse of Cody's experience working with Álvaro Siza Vieira, whose practice concentrates heavily on discussions with the reality of what will occur in the spaces he designs. This questioning goes farther to examine how a whole building works; often, Boyd Cody's projects destabilize the perceived order of traditional spaces, reorienting them to another focus. They are not interested in following a well-known identity for use but in trying to respond to specific sites and landscapes.

Many of the projects on which they've cut their architectural teeth revolved around how an addition can change the old relationship of served/serving spaces in the traditional Georgian Dublin housing stock. Their early projects inculcated Boyd Cody with an ability to "tidy up." Boyd describes the design process as a radicalization of the primary ideas—"we start loose, and the design gets tighter" as they progress, like sharks homing in on a single fish out of a swirling bait ball. They feel theirs is a language that follows certain self-imposed rules, an "etiquette that we understand." These rules then run through the project, avoiding the picturesque in an ordered way. For them it is important to be stating an argument, to make decisions not based primarily on aesthetic considerations but on a persistent logic. Despite this distillation of ideas, their buildings are not simplistic; indeed, the geometric minimalism illustrated in the projects here belies a complexity best understood by experiencing the buildings spatially.

Increasingly, Dubliners are forced to make use of every imaginable space. While some areas of the city are being built unprecedentedly upward as part of a strategic vision for the city, there are swaths of semisuburban Dublin that groan at the seams for new houses. Boyd Cody's Alma Lane House was built at the end of a long back garden of a large Victorian semidetached house, a space seldom used by the owners, in the city's southern commuter suburbs. This is a building as crisp geometric object, a "composition of solid and void," the architects say, which, divorced from the original house and neighborhood pattern, has little to which to answer contextually. The Boyd Cody building had to fulfill the client's seemingly impossible requirements for both privacy and as much natural light as possible. They did indeed surround the house with high stone walls with only the top fifth of the house visible from the street; to solve the light requirement, the architects placed the living spaces on the upper floor. To help further in the pursuit of Ireland's precious natural light, the rooms are not confined to enclosed individuality but left open to one another. To question and then abandon the traditional Irish model of cell-like living spaces below and bedrooms above was not, then, a willful move; it was not Boyd Cody making something strange for the sake of it or exerting their power as architects, but rather a necessary response to the client's needs and the peculiarities of the site.

Richmond Place, say Boyd Cody, was "interpreted into the site" in Dublin. The site for the detached house is at the end of a small street surrounded by modest Dublin two-story terraced housing. Though Boyd Cody was asked to supply two bedrooms and a living space—the "normal" client requirements of a domestic building— they again resisted the impulse to rely on traditional forms. Instead, the design was dictated by the site's constraints. The house fills but limits itself to the boundary line and sinks itself to be in keeping with the height of surrounding houses. Like the Alma Lane house, spaces at Richmond Place flow together, though they are manipulated to allow for more separation than in the previous project. Again, the Platonic forms of the geometry are matched by a disciplined set of materials: brick, aluminum windows, oak, concrete, and rubber. Though the house possesses full height fenestration without the disguising walls at Alma Lane, it does feel private, largely because of the sinking of the building. The living space is enclosed in its site in such a way that it is at once part of the urban fabric of the city and recessed into the domestic.

Their project at St. James, Clontarf, a suburb north of Dublin, is a strange animal. Though it also incorporates huge plate glass, it is, even more than Richmond Place, a decidedly internal project. The geometric addition pulls out from one side of a Victorian

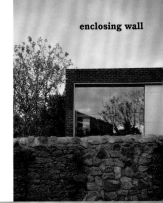

enclosing wall

Paul Tierney

exterior

house, and the new accommodation includes a unified space of living, kitchen, and dining areas. The addition is thus divorced, both spatially and stylistically, from the original house, recentralizing the focus of the overall home. The anonymity of the buildings that frame the house contributes to the project's internalism; so too does the design of the space. Like other Boyd Cody projects, this house employs a continuity in structure and materials: the interior and exterior are rendered in the same material; the floor of the living area becomes the kitchen counter; the floor of the entryway becomes the sill, and then the desk in the dining room. The materials are also kept to a minimal, quiet palette: in-situ concrete, timber framing to plate glass, external render to internal walls. Box-like light scoops create an almost urban landscape on the roof deck and pour illumination, even on Dublin's grayest days, into the space below. This continuity of materials and structure with engineered modes of lighting reiterates the privacy of the space.

The Palmerston Road project makes more vocal its role as an addition to the existing house than its Clontarf relative. The project was meant to provide additional space to the rear of the house, but Boyd Cody interpreted the brief as a reworking of the building's servant areas. Clad, including the roof, in bronze, the new block is a symbiotic object that informs both the interior of the house and gives shape to the spaces in the large garden. This mutually beneficial relationship is evident in the way it enlivens the old house and in the way the bronze folds into the existing house without becoming destructive or parasitic. Being placed above, the kitchen engages with the visual connection of the garden, as does a later development of a studio in the garden. This vantage point will also display how the building changes with the exterior spaces; Boyd Cody carefully chose timber that will gray as the bronze patinates. The hard-finish bronze is complemented in the kitchen and entertainment room below by rubber that coats cabinets, walls, and benches. This is an installation piece: with one move the architects reinvent the rest of what could have been an immovable old dame of Dublin Georgian architecture.

Boyd and Cody are architects who have waived Beckett's right to failure. They question not only seminal issues of typology—"what is a house?"—but also the way each piece of their architecture is made. Spaces fundamental, but also quotidian, to the living of life are not allowed to be less than exceptional. Boyd Cody may achieve "restraint in detail and expression" in the "background of everyday life," as they assert, but this is a simplicity in architecture with considerable depth and breadth. Their designs are too deliberated, too well crafted, to be understood as anything less than complete fluency in design practice and critical reflection about living in Ireland in the twenty-first century.

ground floor plan

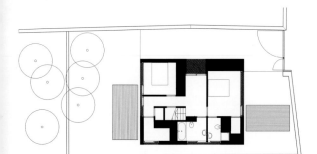

first floor plan

sections

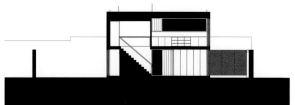

Paul Tierney

Richmond Place

site

Paul Tierney

ground floor plan

first floor plan

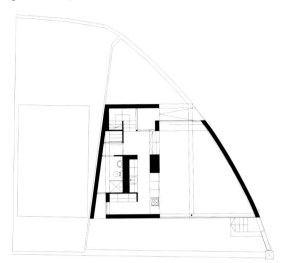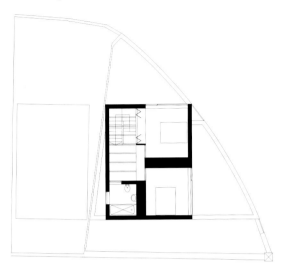

section

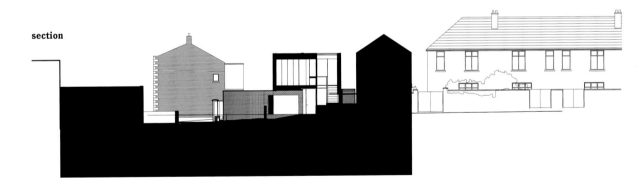

location plan

living space

living space

view to street

Paul Tierney

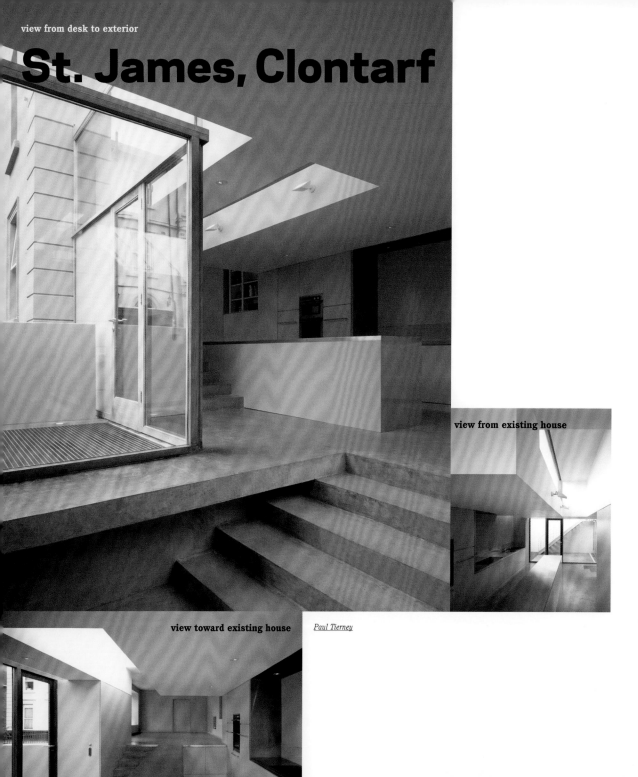

view from desk to exterior

St. James, Clontarf

view from existing house

view toward existing house

Paul Tierney

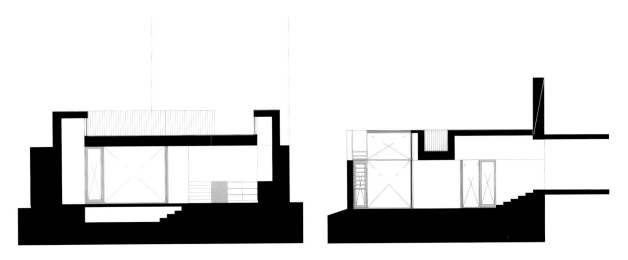

Palmerston Road

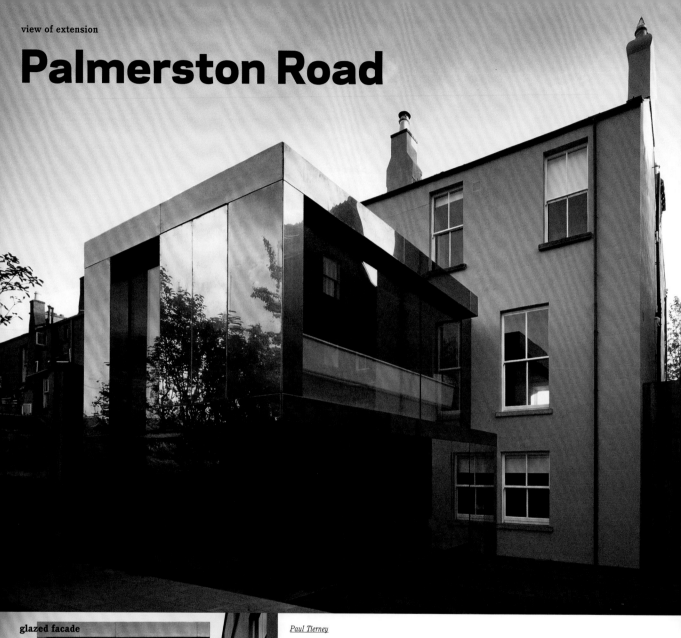

glazed facade

Paul Tierney

Paul Tierney

view from original house into extension

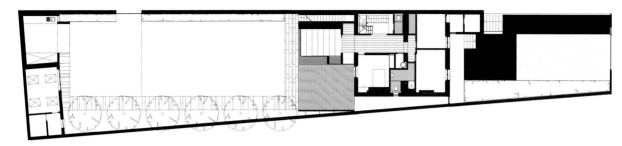

site plan

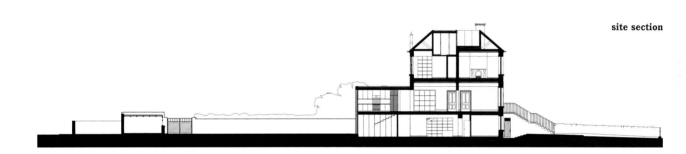

site section

ground floor plan

first floor plan

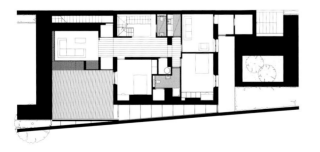

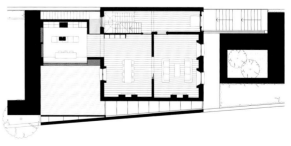

Boyd Cody Architects **31**

view of addition *Alan Jones*

Straidhavern School

Alan Jones Architects

Unlike many architects who left Northern Ireland during the Troubles, Alan Jones thought returning to the region would be a challenge worth taking in architectural terms. After spending ten years with London firms, including Michael Hopkins and Partners, Jones realized that an investigation of a Northern Irish architecture postconflict was not only potentially absorbing but also potentially valuable. With architectural scholar David Brett, Jones scrutinizes the materials, layout, landscape, and construction traditions of the region in their 2007 text, *Toward an Architecture: Ulster Building Our Own Authenticity*. Without producing a definitive answer to their inquiry, the book does resolutely call for a built response specific to the region's cultural and geographic characteristics.

In addition to exploring the landscape and buildings through photography, Jones's practice is heavily influenced by his work teaching at university level. The balance of these methods offers opportunities that cannot be found easily in other modes of practice; the experience of designing and building defines the way he teaches and vice versa.

Jones is particularly skilled at manipulating readily available materials in ways untried and untested in the usually conservative building industry of Northern Ireland. This is nowhere more apparent than at his Straidhavern School project. The existing brick buildings with uPVC windows had to be respected, if not used for inspiration. Jones turned to more industrial solutions for the exterior treatment of the building and, in so doing, provided the rooms with increased daylight through high monopitched roofs. Jones began the project by questioning the brief: was it not possible to provide the school with more flexible space? His solution makes use of a retractable wall between the two adjacent classrooms, furnishing the school with an assembly hall it had never had or expected to be able to afford.

site plan

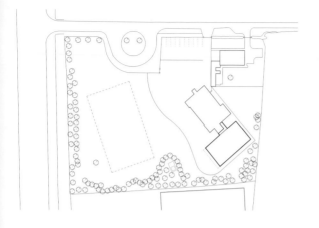

plan

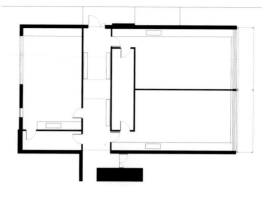

section

The inventive use of materials continues through the most personal of all architectural projects, his own home. Surrounded by buildings redolent with symbolic meaning in Northern Ireland, including a church and a Masonic Hall, the house required a muted external treatment. The barn-like building strangely recedes and then approaches on its site; the roof and walls are covered in a seamless skin of fibrous chipboard roofing material. Many of the interior walls display the unfinished concrete frame whose mold, on the interior, was particleboard; the texture of the composite timber material is left exposed.

Fortunately for Jones, the issues of privacy and sustainability correspond to the site's orientation. The most publicly accessible faces of the house turn north; limited fenestration and less frequently inhabited service areas—utility, cloakrooms, bathrooms—are intelligently configured on the north side of the house. This arrangement not only buffers the living areas from prying eyes but also insulates the colder side of the building. The southern aspect is thus the more outward-looking; views from the full-height canted windows in the main living space not only make use of the best natural southern light but also look out onto the less public garden and stream rather than the road to the front of the site.

These projects represent what architecture in Northern Ireland increasingly is—not simply a deployment of appropriate materials and construction methods but innovative approaches and methodologies to challenging built and cultural problems.

Alan Jones

classroom interior

Jones House

house and surrounding landscape

Alan Jones

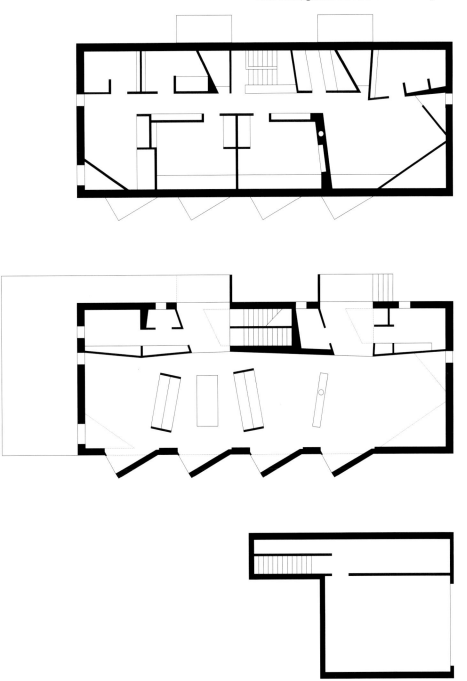

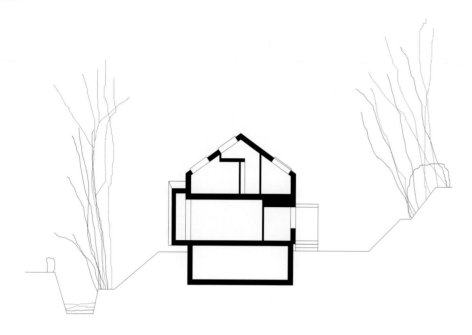

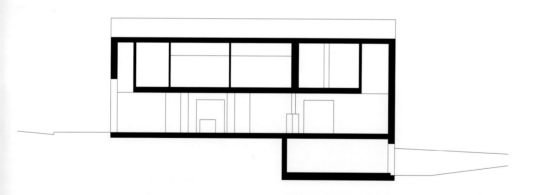

Wooden Building

de Blacam and Meagher Architects

Unlike later waves of Irish architects, de Blacam and Meagher did not spend large portions of their early careers examining the local vernacular, nor did they work on the Continent under the auspices of European architects. Instead both Shane de Blacam and John Meagher worked on the East Coast of the United States for a time—de Blacam with Louis I. Kahn and Meagher for Venturi Scott Brown. The time spent there, particularly with Kahn, is reflected loudly in their built work and in their philosophies about building. They employ simple, elemental forms, evidencing a deep-seated understanding of the resonance of natural materials, particularly timber, and an ability to weave their buildings into the fabric of the urban landscape. Unlike Venturi Scott Brown, though, they do not spend time theorizing about their buildings but demand their architecture stand alone, without rhetoric. Meagher points to the simplicity of the work he and de Blacam

have produced together over thirty years; for him, their architecture is "plain and truthful about what we're making." Structure is often obvious, without pretence. Their project with artist Séan Scully at the entrance to the University of Limerick exemplifies much of this thought: huge, 35-meter-/115-feet-high timber posts and a 760-mm-/2'6"-thick black-and-white-wall in stone are what they say they are—completely solid, heavy, easy to understand, frank.

The Wooden Building, as their residential tower in Temple Bar, Dublin, has come to be known, had significant impact when it was finished in 2000. Situated at the western, quieter edge of the recently rejuvenated and mythologized Temple Bar precinct, de Blacam and Meagher knew that this building demanded substance; they sensed that the dense fabric of the city would withstand a building of several more stories than had been built in the area before. Its timber head rises above the other buildings in the vicinity, but not egregiously so; the firm still maintains the building could have coped with at least two more stories. It feels like a tower in a dense Italian hill town, at once defensive yet legible through the use of expanses of timber.

Like the project at Limerick, this building feels solid and significant. This is again truth to materials; the architects avoid veneer and instead employ depth and thickness that leave no question as to the building's essential elements. In this building, one can easily see the tenet the architects have held throughout their careers: in each project, use the best possible materials the project can afford. The building feels as if it could have been carved out of the existing dense fabric, and indeed, the architects have drawn their elevations in relation to the poché of the surrounding buildings. The building's individual density reflects its environment.

Like many housing projects in Dublin in recent years, de Blacam and Meagher's row of three terrace units at Waterloo Place makes use of a long back garden of an original row. The three houses inhabit the space that would formerly have been given over to only two Victorian homes and, in so doing, create a tighter, more urban answer to housing. The material vocabulary developed in the Wooden Building is repeated here: brick with wide joints, broad expanses of timber, and patinated copper. Here de Blacam and Meagher reflect the material of the surrounding Georgian housing stock with a Lewerentzian burgundy-black brick with thick, pale mortar. The curved green of the roofs sets the terrace apart, but these repeated elements still relate to the urban terrace typology that dominates the area. Thus the materials are different from those used in buildings that surround them, yet the formal moves insert the building into the city fabric without jarring, without shouting "look at me" to their neighbors.

These narrow front and rear elevations and deep plans mean, of course, that light becomes a considerable challenge. Deploying a large window at the top level at the front of the house, a double-height space at the rear, and a spliced roof, the architects ensure that light spills down the white interior walls to infiltrate all circulation spaces. The main living space that inhabits the middle of the three floors makes use, in its open-plan design, of the dual aspect light as well as that which filters down from the rooflights. As a further solution to the illumination problem, the circulation of the building becomes one of its key components. Rather than hide the stair in a corner, de Blacam and Meagher create a narrow, sculptural set of steps that vertiginously makes its way upward into the roofspace, leaving a void at one side for further permutations of light and shadow.

The house called Martha's Vineyard at Dalkey provides a considerable comparison with the Waterloo Road project. The stand-alone house sits in one of Dublin's most prestigious domestic settings, south of the city, with expansive views to Dublin Bay. This is not an urban area of compact terraced housing but a suburban one of single-family homes perched on cliffs above the bay. De Blacam and Meagher's house, however, sits exposed at the water's edge. The architects describe this as a house that had to withstand serious battering by Irish winter weather yet still embrace the drama inherent in a site of this type. They imagine it as a lighthouse, that most durable and functional of buildings that pepper the coast of the country. The house is thus anchored into the rock with an in situ concrete frame cut deeply into the side of the landscape. The walls that emerge out of the sea are granite faced, as are the walls of the entrance block to the house, sited immediately against the road and other neighboring houses. Enveloped by this harder stone is the house's main body, enclosed in more Mediterranean-feeling white rendered walls and huge

Temple Bar context
Peter Cook/VIEW

context

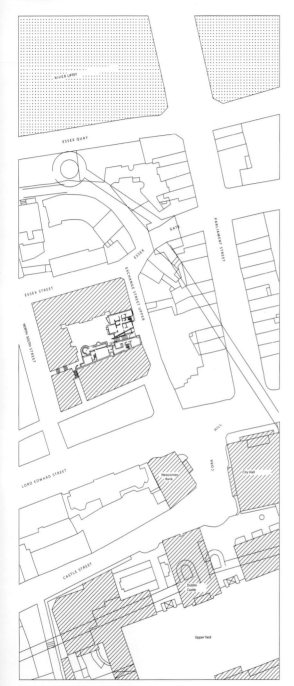

section

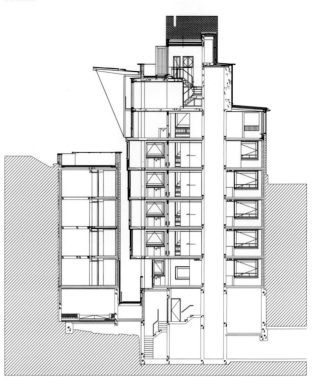

panes of structural glass. A terrace wraps the lower guest level of the house onto which all of the internal spaces open. From there, the house's solidity dissolves into water: first a swimming pool, then a tidal rock pool, and finally the sea itself. With the well-used road and visually busy surroundings of suburban houses on one side and the sometimes roaring sea on the other, the house acts as a pool of quiet.

The new buildings at Cork Institute of Technology represent the culmination of years of work, both for de Blacam and Meagher and for the institution. What began as a new library for the school in the early 1990s then burgeoned into several additional phases, including a catering and hotel school and administration block. The master plan and contingent buildings of the project, developed by de Blacam and Meagher with the Cork office Boyd Barrett Murphy O'Connor, differed from the original plan for the campus with its single, huge arc. Here was an opportunity for the institution to claim a built identity on what previously had been a flat, characterless site, a new entrance for a school without an anchor for its institutional character or built environment.

The new plan creates an urban piazza for the school; the expanse of sky overhead is reflected in the vast deployment of a single material, a space that in the right light alludes to a de Chirico painting. The curve of buildings, with its brick totality, is much larger than the sum of its parts. Brick runs through every massed element, both interior and exterior. Natural light is purposefully deployed onto the brick in internal spaces frequently. Thick cuts into the dense fabric of the buildings create openings in the buildings' elemental geometries. Startlingly for a firm with such a long-standing career and experience in building, this late project strongly recalls the influence of Louis I. Kahn, Alvar Aalto, and Sigurd Lewerentz. There are loud echoes of Saynatsalo Hall, the Philips Academy Library,

and St. Mark's Church throughout the individual buildings and the development as a whole. Rather than drifting away from these heroes of their early career, the Cork Institute exhibits their maintained admiration.

De Blacam and Meagher is the firm to which almost all younger architects point as the source for the current critical interrogation of the way Irish can and should be built, and its work is as persistent and pervasive now as ever. The insistence on solidity has become increasingly robust; one feels, when visiting a work by de Blacam and Meagher, that here is a building designed and fabricated not just for an economic boom or value engineering; it is solidity meant to last for generations.

Mews Houses

context in Dublin

Peter Cook/VIEW

ground floor, first floor, and second floor plans

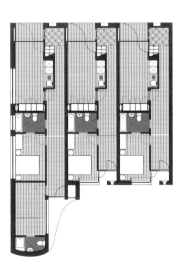
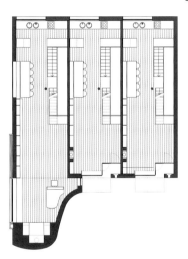
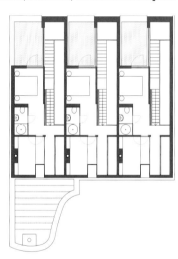

sections

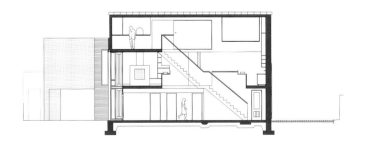
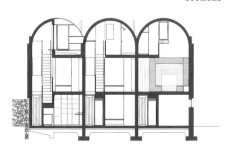

de Blacam and Meagher Architects **47**

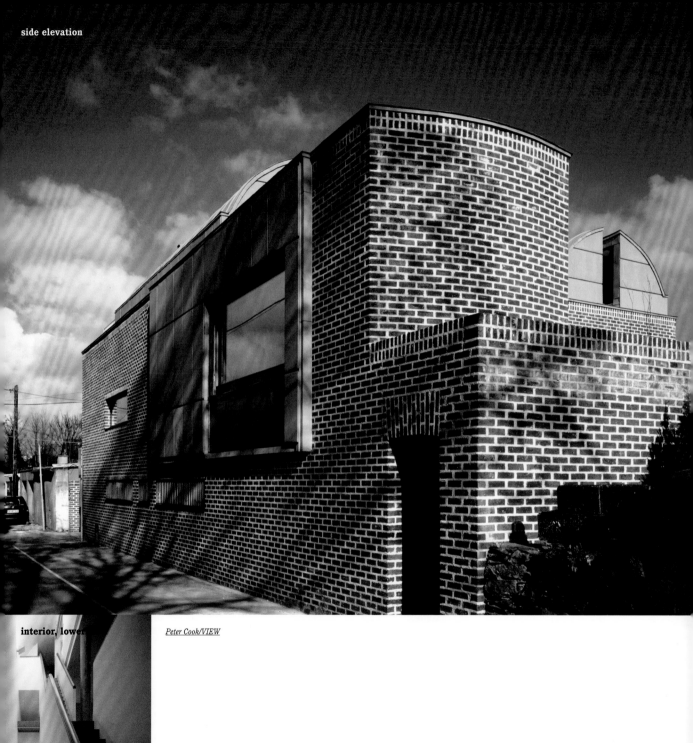

side elevation

interior, lower

Peter Cook/VIEW

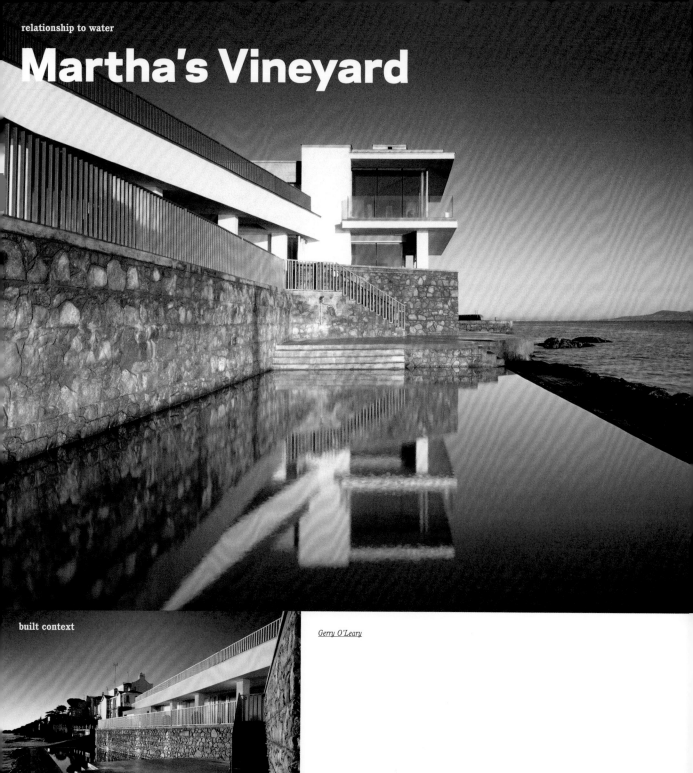

Martha's Vineyard

built context

Gerry O'Leary

Dalkey Island

Martello
Tower

upper ground floor and lower ground floor plans

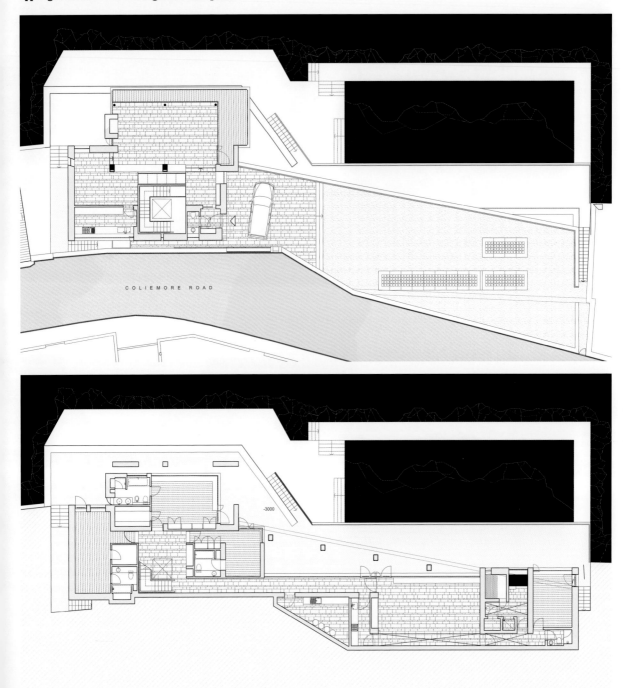

COLIEMORE ROAD

views
to Bay

Gerry O'Leary

interior

courtyard

Cork Institute of Technology

interior materials

main assembly room

courtyard

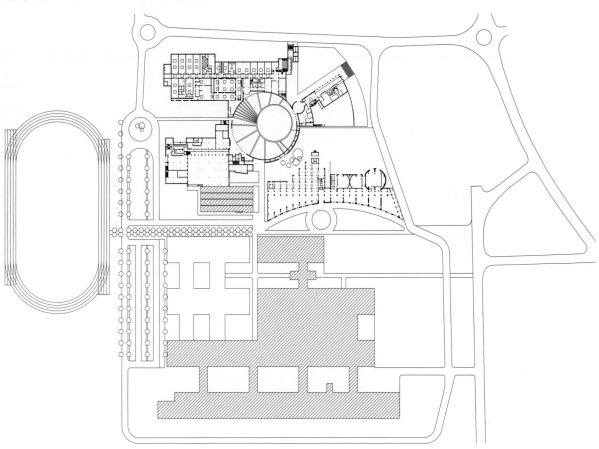

Fingal County Hall

Bucholz McEvoy Architects

Bucholz McEvoy's beginnings, like those of heneghan .peng.architects, has its roots in winning a significant architectural competition. After meeting at Emilio Ambasz's New York office, Merritt Bucholz and Karen McEvoy entered a competition for one of several new council office buildings, this one for the north Dublin suburb of Fingal. In their early thirties, Bucholz, an American, and McEvoy, an Irish native, found themselves moving to Dublin as winners, with the larger firm BDP, of the competition, having beaten a field of 112 other internationally based firms to the post.

With the Fingal win, Bucholz McEvoy were forced to confront scale very quickly: "We never had time to knit small buildings together as so many other practices do," says Bucholz. Despite this lack of the usual experimentation with house extensions or shop fitouts, they believe strongly that even the largest projects are influenced by the individual hands that touch each

component. Not only is this a process that Bucholz McEvoy track with minute care, but it is one on which they feel they must rely.

For Bucholz McEvoy, taking the easy, off-the-shelf answer to architecture is not design. Many of their projects use what seem strange procurement processes within the Irish context; many of their buildings are made off-site where problems can be resolved and valuable time on-site can be saved. They source materials and manufacturers from throughout Europe and are one of the few firms to regularly employ fast-track schedules, common in other parts of the world but only recently beginning to gain utility in Ireland. They are keen to invent new elements, whether structural, as in the timber "boomerangs" at Fingal, or for mechanical and electrical requirements, as in the heat recovery fans employed at their SAP offices. This interest may stem from having worked with Ambasz at a time when his office was producing a vast array of industrial designs; for Bucholz McEvoy, everything can be, and thus should be, designed.

Through their architecture, Bucholz McEvoy seek an expression of what they see as a new Irish society, one with some financial solidity and a cultural blend that has not existed in the past. This new expression is not tied to a particular landscape or building tradition but aligns with the diverse aspirations of a larger society. Bucholz, who was appointed to head the new school of architecture at Limerick, in the west of Ireland, continued this approach in his own teaching and in the pedagogical model for the school. Rather than rely on the traditionally separate studio and lecture system common to most architecture schools, the department was organized around an academy system. It was a deliberate attempt to break down the differences between areas of study to interrogate the underpinnings of architectural education at a basic level.

The importance of the Fingal building is difficult to overstate, both for Bucholz McEvoy as architects and for the context of Irish architecture generally. The building set the bar high for other local councils, and several other buildings with the same typology, including Bucholz McEvoy's civic offices at Dorradoyle, Limerick, have been designed and built to increasingly high standards. The architects did not settle for ready-made components; rather, they solved the problem of creating a structure-free, six-story foyer space with full-height glass wall with the help of Paris-based engineers, RFR. When Bucholz McEvoy talk about the project, they are as likely to show you dozens of photos and drawings of the timber boomerangs that were discarded as the actual building. With this first building, Bucholz McEvoy threw down their gauntlet to declare their commitment to sustainable design. The width of office blocks allows for natural cross-ventilation. Bespoke light fittings project light on the ceiling. Workers are given control over their individual environments with specially designed screened ventilation panels.

The SAP call center offices, located on the outskirts of Galway on Ireland's west coast, follows on from Bucholz McEvoy's desire to represent in architecture a new society in built form, with low energy use and employment of sustainable materials as primary goals of the building. The building's concrete frame supports timber cladding with individually operating timber windows; floor-to-ceiling fenestration and glue-lam beams support a glazed atrium. The office blocks, staggered around the timber-clad atrium space, are each 13 meters wide, allowing for natural ventilation. The structure's concrete mass allows the building to gradually heat up during the day and cool down at night. The building, with its high environmental standards, constant views to external spaces, and pervasive natural daylighting, is not the debased form of call center we have sadly become accustomed to seeing; it is not claustrophobic, mind numbing, or impersonal; it is a space full of natural light and views to the outside.

Maintaining a purist distance from large developers in the building boom that permeated Ireland in the mid-2000s, particularly near Dublin, was not a goal of Bucholz McEvoy. Indeed, creating architecture that was environmentally responsible and innovative with profit-minded, large-scale developers was one of the firm's key successes of that period. Their development of a "mini-city" at Elmpark, to the southeast of Dublin's city center, responds to market demands while addressing environmental concerns with specially designed and made components. Glue-laminated structural elements are used again, with timber cladding and specially sourced glazed panels throughout the hotel, office accommodation, residential units, leisure center, senior citizens housing, day care center, and restaurants. The design for Elmpark, Bucholz says, did not want to cover

front facade

views to Fingal

Michael Moran

offices behind atrium

ground floor plan

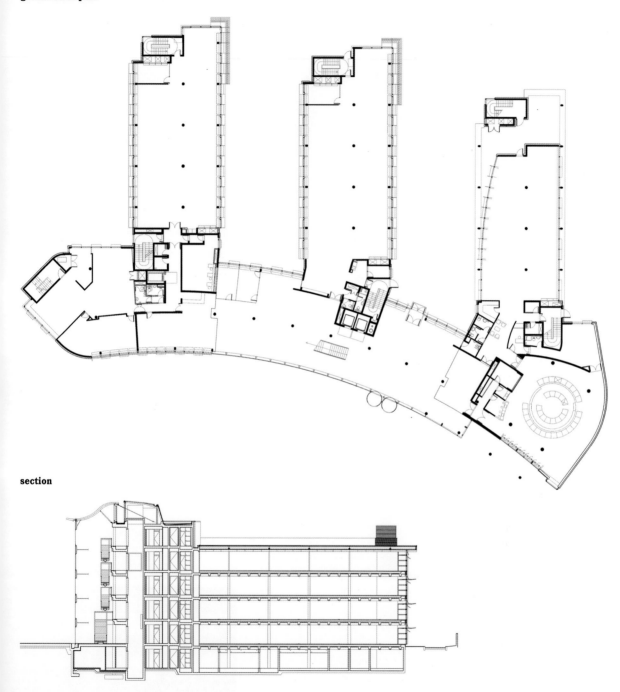

section

up the "bigness." The shared spaces between the buildings make use of the scale of sky and mountains in their response to the landscape into which the new project was inserted. The buildings are in many cases raised off the ground; undersides of polished concrete allow for a flow-through of space, air, and views between the blocks.

In direct contrast to these larger projects, Bucholz McEvoy have also addressed issues of a far smaller scale but with significantly more visibility in several jewel-like pavilions connected to Irish government in the middle of Dublin. Two early projects included the entrance pavilions to government buildings on Merrion Row that acted as precursors for two later projects in the same complex. The welcoming pavilion at Leinster House acts as a controlled entrance not only to the National Museum and Library of Ireland but also to the government buildings of the Republic—"the symbolic memory, knowledge center, and seat of government for the country." The new building acts as an information desk for tourists and as a security point for any visitor or worker entering the complex of buildings; it also operates as a key element in a site redolent with potent symbolism. The tiny buildings play a bewildering number of roles both quotidian and symbolic—gateway, security barrier, busy amenity for workers and visitors, viewpoint for major institutions behind, reflective box of the city, vitrines to display Irish architectural ingenuity and local materials. The pavilion, and its later companion, a shop for the complex, use many of the same technical components being explored by Bucholz McEvoy in other buildings: specially made glazing system and glue-lam larch beams, both of which, being made elsewhere, are installed on site in a matter of weeks and thus follow the firm's interest in the alternative procurement of buildings.

Bucholz McEvoy have an ability, indeed commitment, to engage physically and intellectually with architecture both at its most detailed and wide-reaching scales. They have managed, from the inception of their practice, to maintain a level of detail in their projects, no matter the size, speed of construction, or client type. This exists alongside their insistence on specially designed components or materials in a context of a building industry known for its multiple housing units. Their projects are also often located within realms of considerable symbolic potency while creating spaces of the highest quality in which to work and live. They manage to confront the full gamut of what architecture can and should be, not only the architecturally specific through detail, structure, environmental performance, and design but also in the social, political, and economic issues with which architecture, thankfully, is so inextricably embedded.

SAP Building Galway

atrium

Michael Moran

lobby

Michael Moran

waiting area

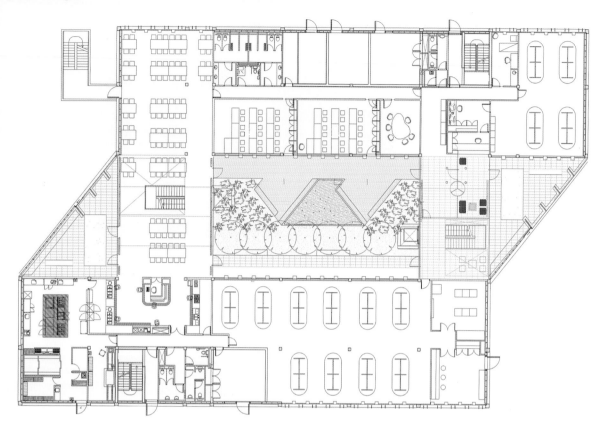

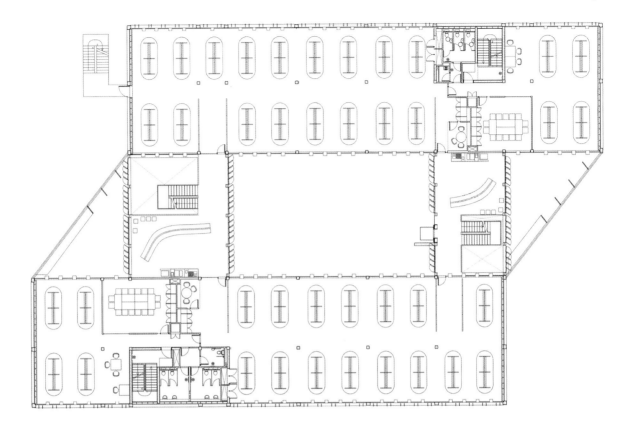

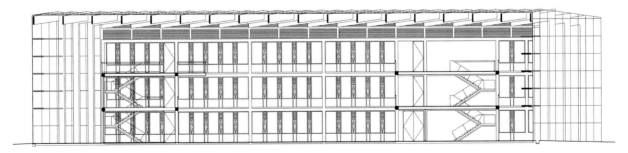

Elmpark

hotel

Michael Moran

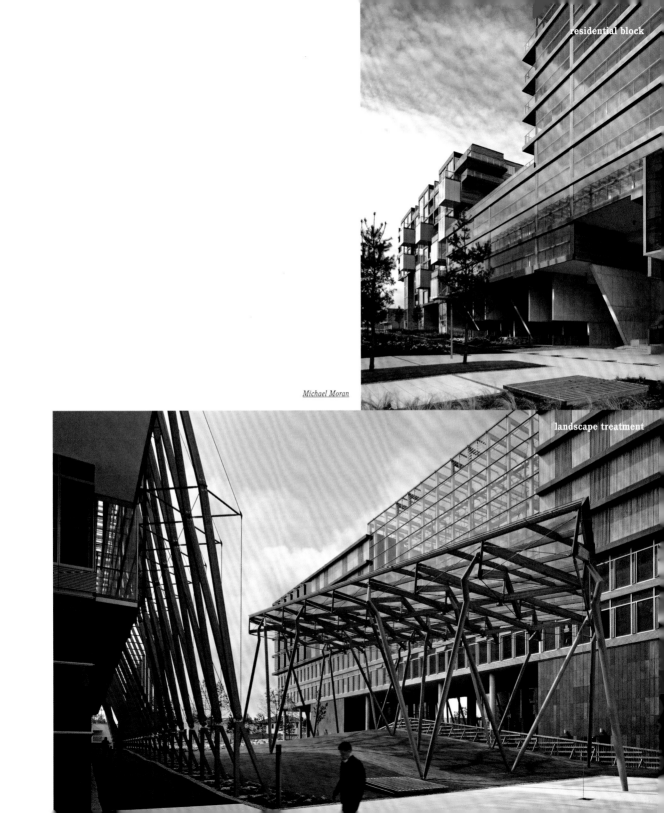

Michael Moran

site plan

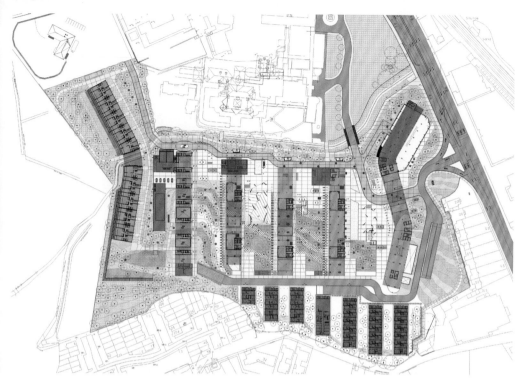

site section

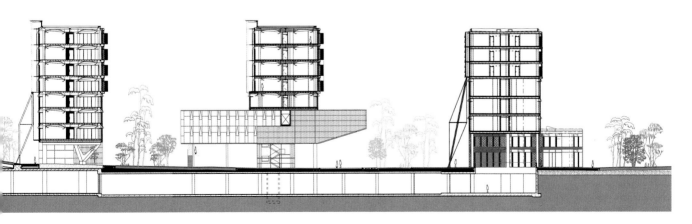

Leinster and Siopa Pavilions

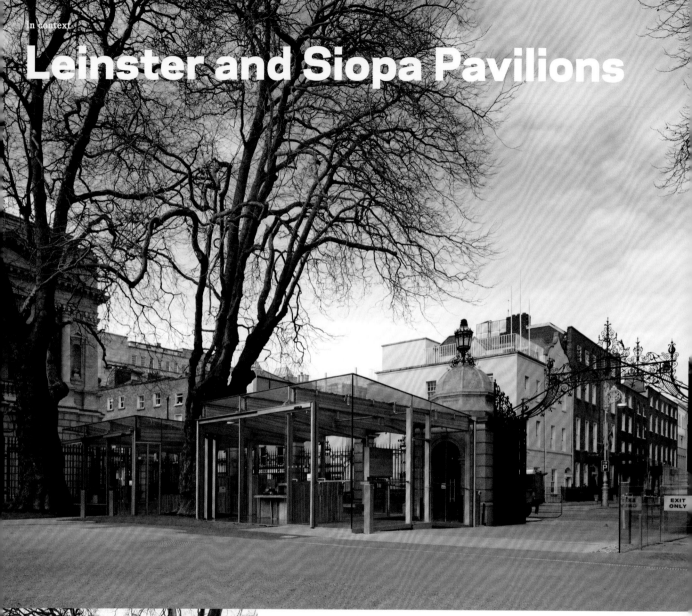

Michael Moran

security pavilion plan

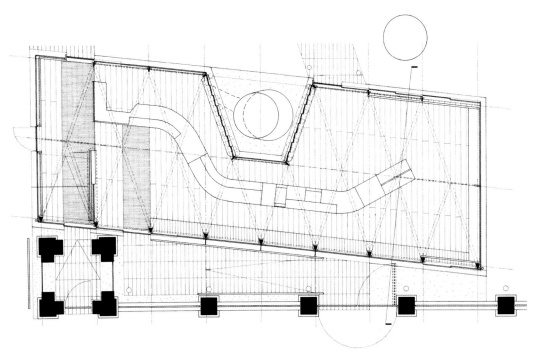

security pavilion long section

security pavilion short section

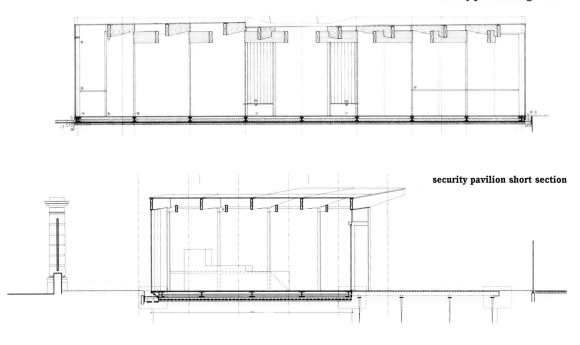

shop plan

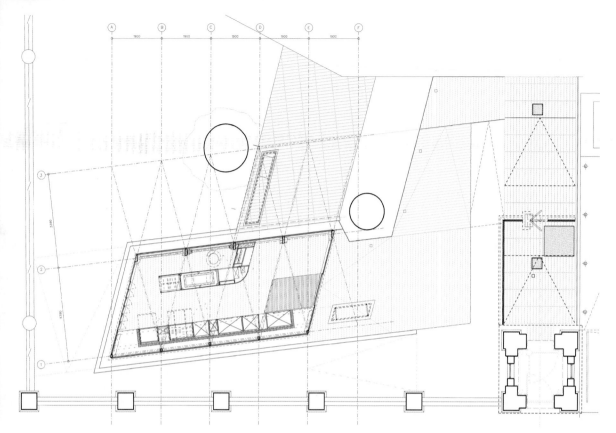

Michael Moran

de Paor Architects

De Paor Architects is a firm with a considerable following. "I'm in love with this house," Kenneth Frampton said of their Wallpaper project in Cork.[1] Tom de Paor won *Building Design* magazine's Young Architect of the Year Award in 2003. Irish critic and curator Shane O'Toole has no hesitation in avowing that "de Paor's is the most original talent to emerge in Irish architecture in the past 10 years."[2]

De Paor Architects' approach to architecture includes the pursuit of sculpture and object. In his early career de Paor drew inspiration from the practice of artists and spent a year as architect in residence at the National Sculpture Factory in 1993–94, in Cork, before receiving a commission there to insert an intervention into the main shed space. His works, particularly the early examples, have been called "buildings as utensils, as furniture, scaleless,"[3] and de Paor states that he sometimes "suppresses the detail to achieve that object-like quality." He often discusses the materiality of his projects before programmatic solutions or relations to site; it is the ability to combine this interest in the object with the pursuit of sophisticated spatial solutions that makes the firm's work remarkable.

This attitude toward buildings contrasts with de Paor Architects' interest in large-scale projects such as its master plan for an area in East London centered on an arterial route through the area. The master plan called for the redesign of moments around particular junctions on the A13 road. De Paor collaborated with two artists on a "light garden." This was a project based in kilometers, one that would orchestrate the experience of thousands of drivers every day. Perhaps both of these approaches to architecture are indeed scaleless as others have suggested, the same type of scalelessness that one perceives at once under a microscope and in examining the distances between planets.

Many of de Paor Architects' moves and interests seem to tend toward the Baroque—a sense of wit, concealment, inhabiting density, carving out of space, an interest in surface, the choosing or inventing of a theme, then endlessly playing with it, both within a single theme and in a series of related projects. The spaces often have looping routes created through spaces with siphoning walls that cause the user to move through in a non-hierarchical manner replete with choice.

De Paor Architects' entry to represent Ireland at the Venice Biennale in 2000 is one of those extremely rare projects that has resonance as well as humor. In representing Ireland, the firm wanted to build a structure that was small and modest in cost, but evocative of both an ancient and contemporary society. The peat industry in Ireland, while often ignored as antiquated, has an enormous impact on the landscape and energy use of the country; peat bogs cover 16 percent of the island. Used as fuel for open-hearth fires as well as in a major electricity generation plant, peat comes in several forms. The most commonly known are peat briquettes, which are a compressed, smokeless version of the fuel. De Paor Architects engineered 1,676 of these ubiquitous, every-day bricks into a trapezoidal structure, what de Paor called a "sensory pavilion and speculation on land," evoking, among other things, the dwellings and small stone churches of Ireland. It could be inhabited by only a few people at a time, in direct contrast to the enormous sheds and specifically designed pavilions assembled by other participating countries. Not only was it an "architecture that smell[ed,]"[4] but one with a calorific value (373,782 MJ) and listed sulfur content.

The substation project at Clontarf, just to the north of Dublin's Conolly train station, seems to conflate earlier works of de Paor Architects—its pursuit of architecture as object, but also the enormous scale of urban reconfiguration shown in the A13 project. The design for the site includes the building as well as a significant amount of new landscaping, which reorchestrates the area with protective berms of precast concrete for a gridded network of new trees and bespoke lampposts. The building sits in the promenade park at the water's edge, at the T-junction of Clontarf's two main streets; the project is meant to reinform and shift the focus of the somewhat mundane intersection.

The prepatinated copper-shingled building itself is made up of three programs: recladding an existing pumping station, a maintenance equipment store, and an electricity substation. This is a mysterious building: repeated circumnavigations of the freestanding structure do not give any clues to its purpose. The in situ concrete frame is covered in copper shingles, punctuated by Iroko timber screens that have transformed to gray over time. Every element of the exterior shell objectifies the building: the flush doors with recessed handles, the corners over which the shingles wrap continuously, the minimal concrete plinth, and a single high-level window that does not allow for a view into the interior of the building. Though it is an object of a certain size, it is difficult to come to terms with its scale; one can't discern the building's use, enter the building, or see into its space to get a better idea of the possible human interaction with it.

The sculptural note also pervades de Paor Architects' commission for the Irish Aid, an arm of the Irish government's Department of Foreign Affairs. The retrofit of a 1960s office building on the north end of one of Dublin's main thoroughfares, O'Connell Street, seeks to show the public how government funds are spent on aid to foreign countries. For de Paor Architects, the project immediately embraced the notion of projection of images as the most persuasive and accessible method of display. They begin with the skin of the building: rather than follow the original building line, the glazed facades

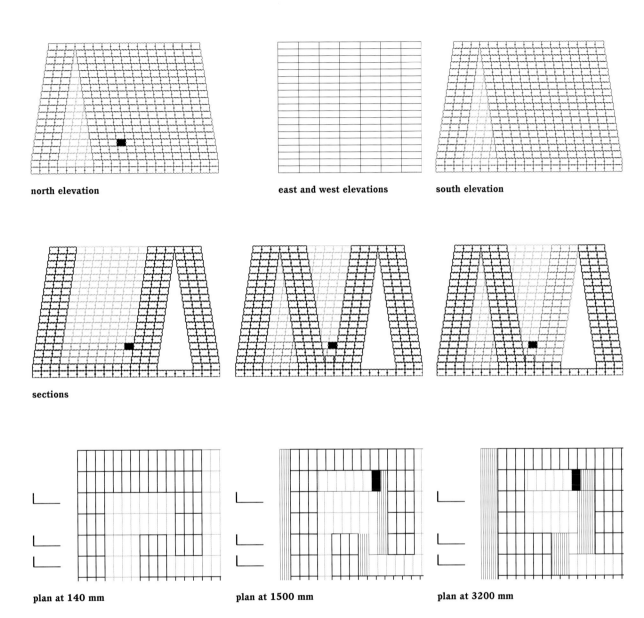

north elevation

east and west elevations

south elevation

sections

plan at 140 mm

plan at 1500 mm

plan at 3200 mm

exterior *Dennis Mortelli*

construction *de Paur Architects*

entrance
Dennis Mortelli

hinge inward and back out again, inviting a passerby into what would have been the interior of the building to seek images on the white walls of the interior space. The existing space, riddled with a dense forest of in-situ concrete posts, is carved into a series of enclosed spaces dictated by the needs of projection of images. The angles required by the equipment and wall space for projection dictate the location of walls, ceiling heights, and materials. Here we see the deployment of areas into which a variety of activities can be funneled, though in this case usually centered on the viewing of images. Spaces encourage the viewer not only to follow a particular sequence but also to wander among the planes. De Paor also employs a series of vertical levels, from bench to coat rail to ceiling heights, that hide the building's significant wiring and ventilation needs. The result is another exploration of the poché—an incredibly dense, almost solid space with methods of passing-through carved into a simple palette.

The office also remains committed to exploring the house as object. In a series of projects originally called the 10 x 10 x 10, each house is square on plan, approximately 10 meters by 10 meters. Depending on the location, the elevational design changes as do the materials of the external envelope and roofscape. In each case, the house's internal configuration is structurally flexible and in some cases open plan. In the specimen shown here built in Connemara, on the west coast of Ireland, the plan is divided into a large, open-plan living area with modest bedrooms opening directly onto the living space; each bedroom also has its own access to the landscape. The external envelope reflects the area's local stone, while the interior is treated with horizontal boarding, all of which might have another permutation in another location.

These buildings relate to both the vernacular, two-story farmhouses that sit alone in the landscape of Ireland while borrowing from purely modernist ideas of rectiliniarity—a theme not often seen in de Paor's work to date. They are not modular buildings but speak to the infinite possibilities of a single elemental form sitting on different sites. This Baroque variation on a theme allows de Paor and his office to play with plan and cope with the self-imposed strange scale relationship, seen in previous projects, that a totally square building brings to its site. Future projects, one suspects, will continue the interrogation, with increased variation, of these issues of object, scale, and event in their architecture.

1 "Soft Shell: Thomas de Paor's Interlocking Moves," *Building Design BD Ireland*, 17 March 2000, 15.
2 Shane O'Toole, "Art to Drive By," *Sunday Times,* 14 May 2000.
3 Gerry Cahill, "The Doors Were Left Open," *Irish Architect* 152 (November–December 2000): 62.
4 Shane O'Toole, "The Irish Pavilion at the Venice Biennale," *Irish Architect* 160 (September 2000): 12.

street side elevation

Clontarf

water side elevation

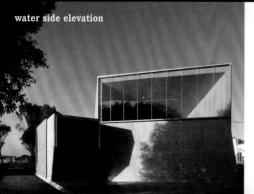

interior

Dennis Gilbert/VIEW

detail of elevation

site plan

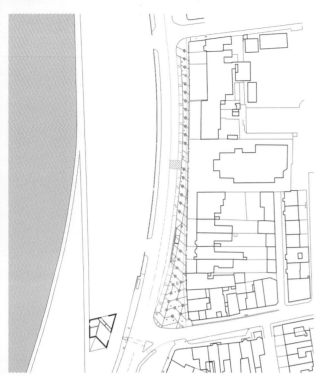

continuous site section

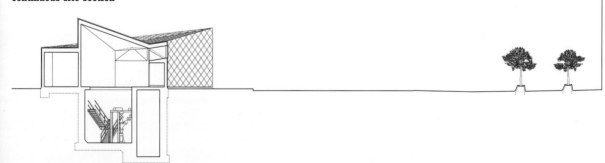

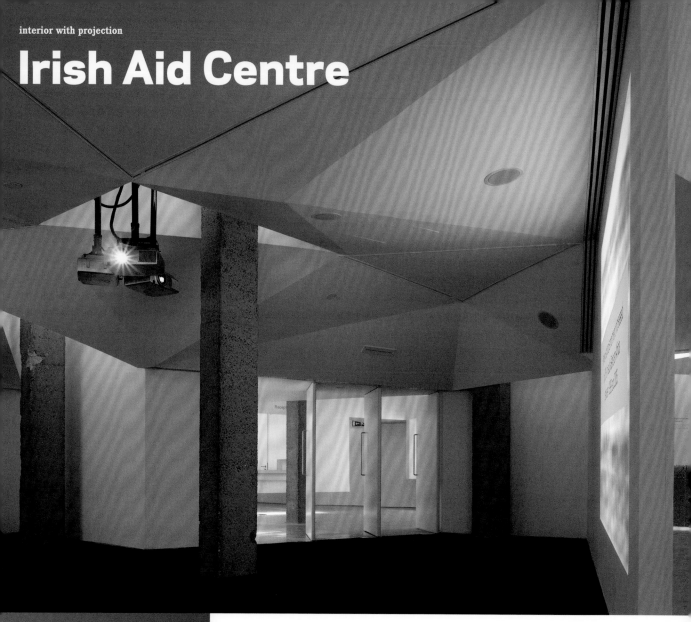

interior with projection

Irish Aid Centre

interior

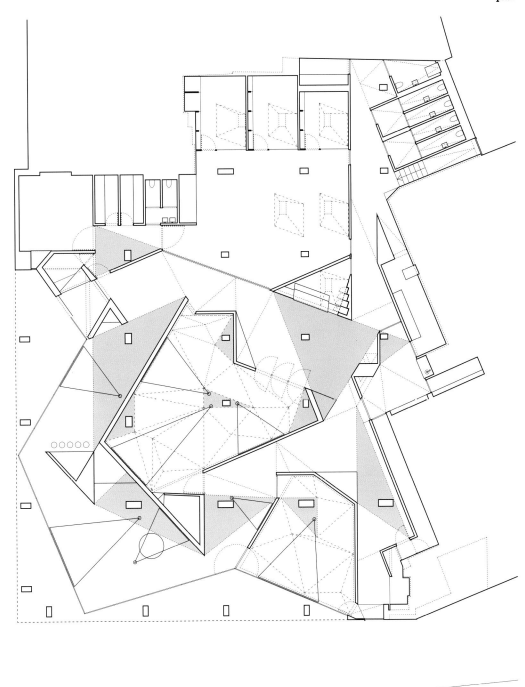

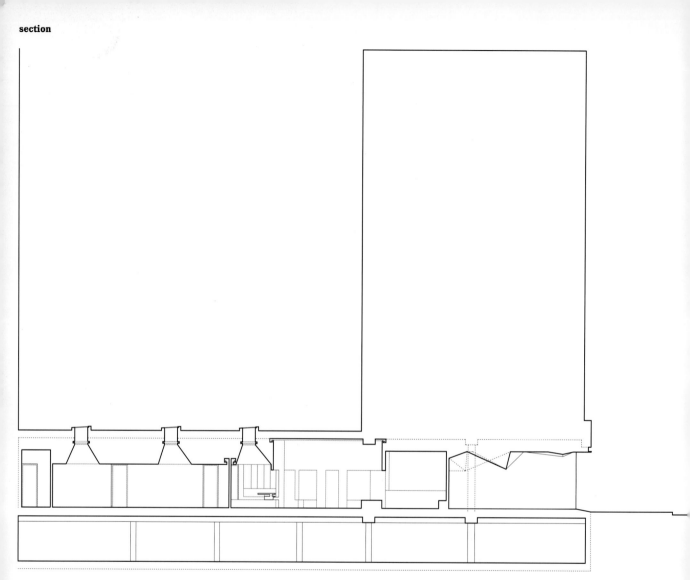

view from street

Teach Adhuain

kitchen

Nelson Carvalho

Nelson Carvalho

ground floor plan

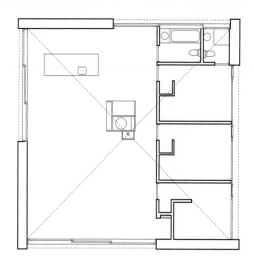

section

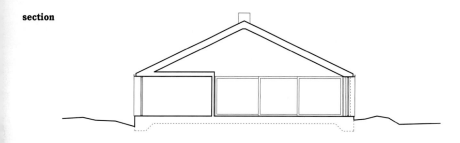

elevation

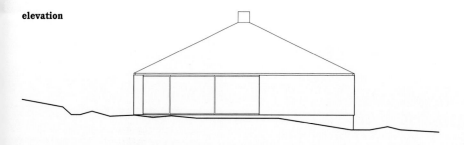

facade *Hélène Binet*

S3

FKL Architects

For Michelle Fagan, Paul Kelly, and Gary Lysaght, an architectural project can and should begin with a single cohesive idea, one that answers any and all questions throughout the design, detailing, and on-site life of the project. While the design concept can change over time as the designers' understanding of the site, the client, and the programmatic requirements develops, it is nonetheless essential to their whole process of making architecture. For every project, too, this concept can be described in a simple diagram. It answers questions of materiality, how light should enter a room, and what means of circulation will be utilized, and it translates into a reduction of moves and materials.

FKL Architects declare they have a decidedly "humane and holistic" interest in the spaces they create. It seems that creating successful architecture for FKL is the design of spaces that are both interesting to build and a joy in which to live and work; its buildings also reinforce individuality and make more apparent their surroundings. The buildings are also sensitive to their environmental impact; after curating the Irish Biennale 2006 SubUrban to SuperRural, the firm's work has become increasingly concerned with environmental issues affecting Ireland. The strong admiration of the Georgian street facades that dominate many parts of Dublin derives from an affinity to their stripped-down essence, but Georgian rooms also make the most of sunlight, ensure natural ventilation, and have direct connection to the city in which they sit.

The S3 office building was the second new building in four years for a computer company client because of rapidly increasing staff numbers. The clients were, on the one hand, willing to gamble on a young firm for the building, and FKL, in turn, was prepared to create a building that did not continue the sad history of bland, oppressive workplaces in suburban office parks. FKL understood the main distinction of spaces as those "private" work areas and "public" gathering spaces, including a foyer, atrium, and auditorium. The overarching design concept, then, began with a generic block with these public spaces removed or chipped away to articulate the different spaces. The building feels like a preexisting form that has been carved into by the architects; smooth black panels of reconstituted stone are cut to reveal the public spaces in a contrasting lighter color and rougher texture. FKL's decision to highlight the public spaces—circulation, entry, lobby—indicates its aspiration to celebrate these areas of interaction and exchange.

Set on a highly visible corner site, FKL's extension and renovation to the Baldoyle Library adds a new entrance, local government office, gallery, and workshop space to an existing library in one of Dublin's northern waterfront commuter suburbs. To quietly signal the building's public status, FKL devised a rectilinear form that contrasts with the existing adjacent houses. FKL took the opportunity here to invigorate the public space in front of the building as well. In paving the formerly lackluster space, FKL not only provides an announcement of entry to the building but also gives the suburban Baldoyle community a potential center for public use.

The overarching idea for the building was to provide a "manipulated tube" of new space around the existing library, much of which was to act as circulation. The "tube" is constructed from in-situ concrete; the exterior of the building is clad in quiet gray stone. On the interior, the concrete can be read on all surfaces—floors, walls, and ceilings. Individual areas with different uses are then made distinct from one another, clad in Iroko timber. One enters on the new mall side of the building with direct access down a new corridor into the older building in which the library now sits. However, if one turns to either side, one finds ceiling-height glazed spaces that overlook the seafront, on the ground floor, and in the upper workshop room, over the beach and Dublin Bay beyond. The building thus begins and ends with the view out to sea, the focus of the town. With the clad-tube design concept, the Baldoyle Library is a building that has many chapters; materials change, different views open to both interior and exterior, and a variety of uses is accommodated.

The Reuben Street Apartments act as a significant and much-needed marker for the city of Dublin, an attempt to give identity to one of the main routes into the city center as it becomes enveloped in new higher-density development. The site, located on what was formerly the outer limit of the old city, is an area where the traditional one- and two-story shops and housing are no longer economically viable in the Dublin of the early twenty-first century. Here, the building is conceived as two L-shaped units of housing atop what FKL calls an "articulated landscape" of entry and semipublic courtyard spaces.

The high-density building emerges out of the traditional landscape, rising to twelve stories at one corner; as a new type of housing for the area, the block required careful treatment by the architects. They were intent not only on providing a large-scale building but on preserving a sense of individuality. The seventy apartments do not monotonously repeat one another in plan or elevation, and each unit is lit from more than one side. That residents are able to identify their own apartments from the street via the changing fenestration further enhances this notion of individuality within a large building. The goal of maintaining a connection to the local environment is pursued both through a courtyard at ground level and especially in a communal roof garden that allows the tower's inhabitants to locate themselves within the city.

facade inset *FKL Architects*

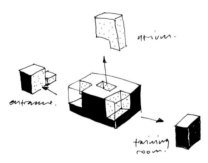

atrium.

entrance.

training room.

concept sketch

entry *Cillian Hayes*

approach

interior

Hélène Binet

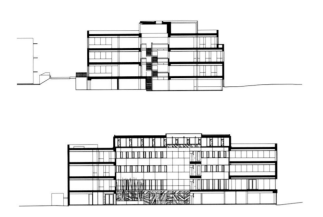

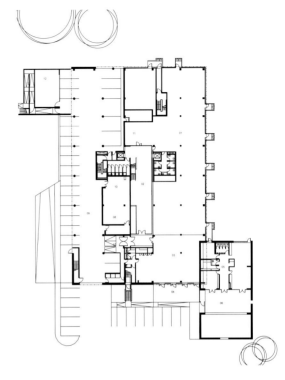

In the Howth House, many of FKL's previous ideas are brought to increasing fluency. Here again is the sensitivity to a remarkable site, the use of polished precast concrete used with effect at S3, again the deployment of a design concept that invigorates the design process and the final building. At Howth, the building responds to a client's needs for privacy while making best use of the site, which includes views of surrounding heather-covered hills, Dublin, and the Irish Sea. The upper story overlooks the site and houses the building's more public functions—reception, kitchen, office—while the bedroom area below feels more discreet and inward turning. The public spaces above can be opened fully into one another to create flowing space, but the quieter sleeping spaces maintain their independence. This does not become two separate buildings, however, as the architects have insisted on continuity of finish throughout. For example, the open-plan nature of the

upper story can be configured with doors that become walls, which then transform rooms into seamlessly lined walnut boxes; Italian marble used in areas of the lower story was chosen specifically to enable the veins in the stone to run continuously on the walls.

For FKL, the use of an overarching design concept enables it to deploy, indeed insist, on this level of detail in its buildings. A distinct idea strongly stated at the inception of the project then demands that all aspects of the design be interrogated, and no arbitrary decisions are made. After Venice, FKL is putting into practice a broad-ranging definition of sustainability by reducing waste, in materials, and in incorrect moves. FKL's architecture is not about the pursuit of beauty but about the truth and legibility that a building can produce.

view from seafront

Baldoyle Library

new public space

Paul Tierney

Paul Tierney

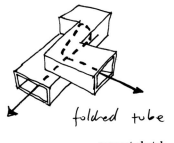

concept sketch

ground floor and first floor plans

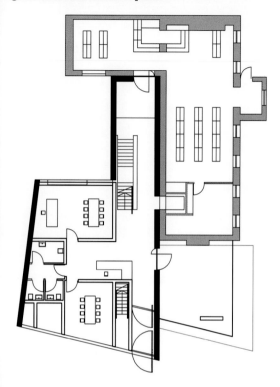 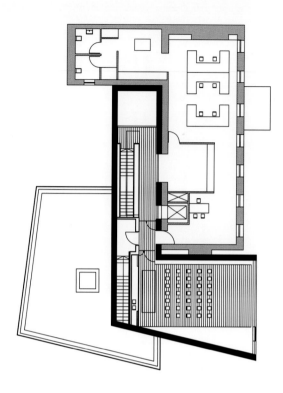

site section

Reuben Street Apartments

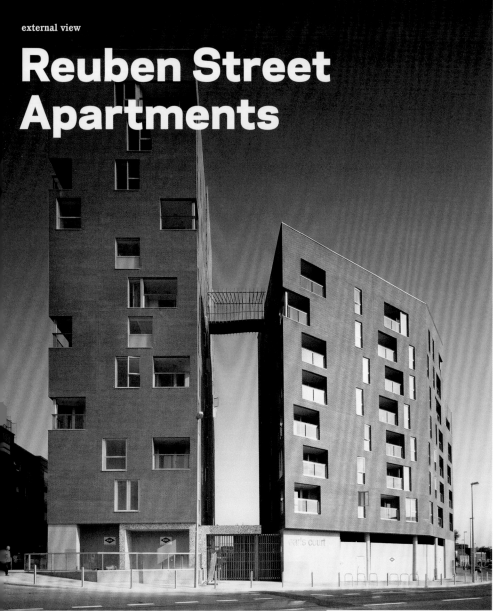

distant view

Paul Tierney

concept sketch

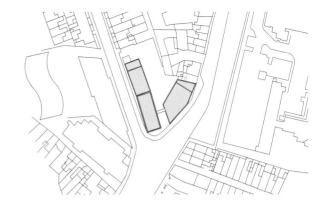

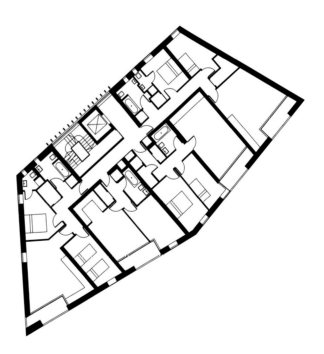

Howth House

hillside facade   *Verena Hilgenfeld*

Verena Hilgenfeld

concept sketch

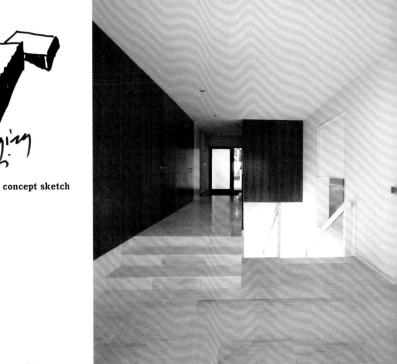

ground floor and first floor plans

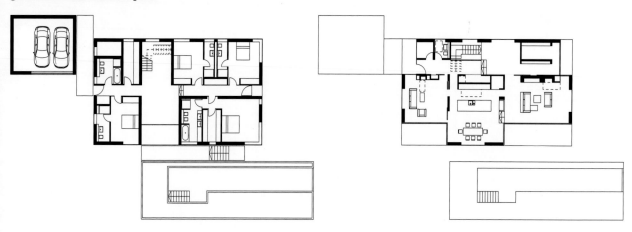

sections

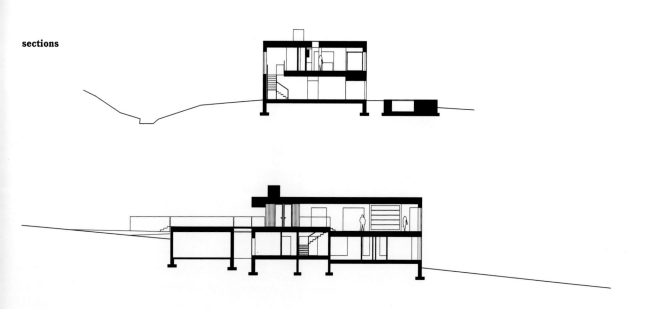

In Between House

Dominic Stevens Architect

The résumé of Dominic Stevens includes the following manifesto: "I run a one person practice from a truck container in a field in rural Ireland. I divide my time between architecture, caring for my children and growing organic food. I carry out one building project at a time informed by ongoing theoretical work. My work evolves as a series of firmly held beliefs tempered by practice." After years working in Berlin and Dublin, Dominic Stevens decided in 1999 to relocate his life, family, and practice to rural south Leitrim, and as such represented the first influx of new families to move into the area in more than a generation.

As his manifesto suggests, architectural practice for Stevens is directly connected to the method by which he lives his life: his house, working methods, and immediate environment are all essential to his practice of architecture. Most projects in which he has been involved center on the scale, materiality, setting, and questioning of the domestic sphere. An early entry to the Architectural Association of Ireland's annual awards was not a single house but a system for intervention into the existing Dublin housing stock he calls "domestic acupuncture." His first book, *domestic*, was published in 1999, and his research as part of the Kevin Kieran Award and bursary for architectural research resulted in the book *rural,* published in 2007.

As can be expected with his commitment to research, Stevens is gathering examples of alternative ways of living in a catalog of recent Irish vernacular architecture, "built slowly, cheaply, without mortgages." His own house, built with the help of friends and students in timber frame, makes use of recycled materials from several locations. Stevens is quick to point out that even his specially commissioned projects have been built for "less than the standard bungalow." He uses everyday, often agricultural means of building in untried ways: one

111

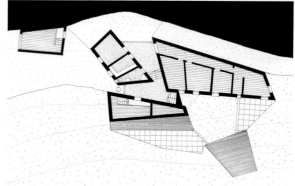

house extension used a precast concrete fencing system, rotated 90 degrees to run horizontally, in its main structural walls.

Stevens thinks about domestic architecture in terms of its functions by specific individuals within particular landscapes. The In Between House, set in the Leitrim countryside, could have looked like that quintessential "Oirish" cottage. Instead, Stevens turns the stereotype on its head, both formally and programmatically. Using the same white render and dark roof common to so many countryside dwellings, he configures the house into a new set of geometries. Further, the house is composed of two different types of spaces—those with a recognizable shape in which there is no question one is in a "room," and other, more remarkable "in between" spaces, where unplanned domestic life can happen. These rooms are not bedrooms, dining rooms, or kitchens but nebulous, unpremeditated areas of the house.

The Mimetic House—unlike the traditional white cottage, or the transplanted Spanish bungalows that have lately encroached on Ireland's rural landscape—hides itself in its environment in dually opposed above- and below-ground spaces. Its upper floor is wrapped in mirrored panels and is roofed in sebum, dissolving the house into its environment. Half of this house occurs below ground, buried in the landscape. In the main upper room, every other wall panel is a solid while its neighbor gives a canted floor-to-ceiling view of the landscape outside. In this dual opposition, the Mimetic House reflects a tendency in many of Stevens's houses—quieter spaces are carved below the more public, usually light-filled areas that perch above.

Stevens works outside the mainstream of both Irish architecture and architectural culture in general. His thinking about his practice is careful, but simultaneously rational and unusual. This alternative take on both formal decisions and his practice of architecture results in ideas that may very well have some of the strongest resonance for a new, reconfigured Ireland.

Ros Kavanagh

in between space on stair

Mimetic House

house in context

views from upper floor   *Ros Kavanagh*

unfolded interior elevation

upper level plan

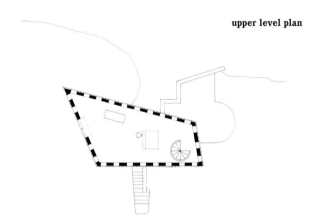

section

lower level plan

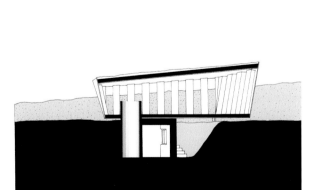

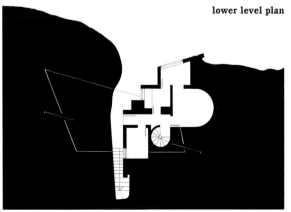

Dominic Stevens Architect **115**

Urban Institute

Grafton Architects

Anthropologist Clifford Geertz developed the notion of "thick description" as a method of observation that features both description and analysis. One examines not only the subject but also its context and motivations that influence actions and behavior. Yvonne Farrell and Shelley McNamara, the founders of Grafton Architects, display an uncanny facility for a "thick description" for architecture—a seemingly innate ability to connect with the specificity of the place in which they work for each project. In conversation, they relate that it is often the small, ordinary events and objects that are most informative. This perception, these antennae for rapidly grappling with and understanding a location, is elemental to their pursuit of finding a "language that has meaning" for each building they produce. They and their firm have honed this skill in Ireland in seeking an Irish architecture, particularly in light of Kenneth Frampton's arguments for a critical regionalism; they

have recently found that their facility transfers beyond their familiar ground.

Farrell and McNamara studied together and founded their firm only three years after completing university. Their design for Temple Bar Square was key to Group 91's transformation of the Temple Bar area of Dublin. Many of the architects in this volume point to Farrell and McNamara's teaching or time spent in Grafton Architects' offices as seminal to their development as architects.

The Urban Institute at University College, Dublin, houses the many types of academics who work in the field of the urban environment—planners, architects, environmental experts, geographers. Among this bewildering myriad of users, Grafton Architects not only had to question the site and institution into which the buildings would be implanted but also interrogate carefully the nebulous brief; here brief making became a key part of their sketch design. This is a building that the architects compare to a tartan cloth. The weaving takes place across many levels—in the manner in which this new addition fits with its older neighbors, in the combination of a heavy base and lighter terracotta tiles in the external treatment, in plan and section, and, perhaps most importantly, in how the building's users work together.

To facilitate a cross-pollination of expertise, Grafton Architects did away with the usual long corridors to which cell-like offices are appended as afterthoughts. Instead, the building is organized around striations of space. Rooms feed into one another, though they can be separated by sliding doors or the occasional timber-clad wall. Each room allows for cross views, encouraging light and activity into unexpected spaces. The section is as varied as the plan: standing in one area of the building allows for views above, across, and below. The building hums with students, researchers, and faculty constantly crossing paths, exchanging ideas. This building, one suspects, gets better with time, as the users exploit their space and fill it with evidence of their communal work and exchange.

Like McCullough Mulvin's Source Art Centre and Library in Thurles, the Solstice Arts Centre at Navan, in County Meath, is another surprise of a building in a small, traditional Irish town. The center sits on a difficult, sloping site with its main facade presenting onto Navan's ring road; this is an effort by the community to instill a new center for an expanding town. At its inception, the building was, tantalizingly, to house both a theater for revolving users and the local courts. In the middle of the design process, however, the courts were removed, and an exhibition space supplanted it.

The busy ring road is met with a long glass facade that angles along the existing street line and wraps around to a new public space at the building's entrance. Behind that facade stretches the foyer/café space, treated in quiet gray travertine flooring with raw concrete walls. The black marble of the box that tops the building can be seen again in the foyer's ceiling. This is a space for more than meeting and drinking coffee: the long wall opposite the glass facade acts as a singular display space, allowing visitors to preview exhibitions that can be seen upstairs. The galleries, which inhabit the upper stories of the building, incorporate both interior and external "sky gardens" for the display of outdoor pieces or events. The refrigerated, sterile, white box approach has not happened here; each of the gallery spaces varies from the one that leads into it, and all are lit by natural lighting with natural ventilation.

The main focus of the building, however, is the theater space. Because of site constraints and natural slope, Grafton Architects decided to arrange the seats as an asymmetrical interior landscape. This allows for a more intimate relationship between audience and performers but also creates a seating space that can be as intriguing to witness as the activity on stage. The architects further question the norms of "auditorium" by allowing in both foyer-borrowed and direct natural light. This space, which recalls Aalto's outdoor amphitheaters, breathes asymmetrical urbanity into the heart of the building.

The firm won the competition to extend Milan's Bocconi University, representing a major milestone in Irish architecture: in addition to heneghan.peng .architects' win in Egypt, it is one of the first significant foreign competitions to have been won by an Irish firm. Grafton Architects' "thick" and informed response to the site, its ability to understand the essence of the local context, was a major factor in its winning the design, coupled with its capacity to solve the client's difficult requirement for a bifurcated auditorium.

For Grafton Architects, the project answers the need for specific programmatic requirements, including a new three-story research library, a 1,000-seat dividable

stair

studio space

Ros Kavanagh

work spaces

ground floor plan

upper floor plan

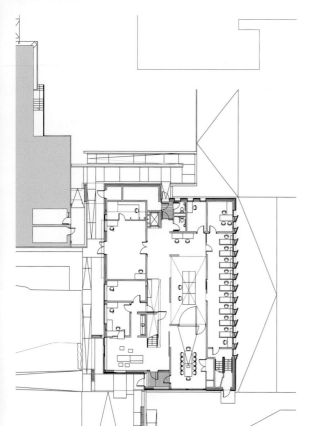

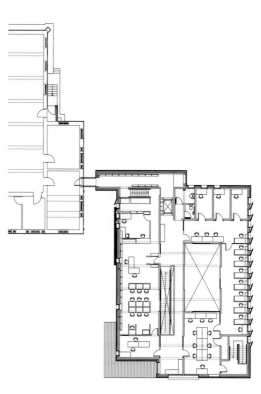

section

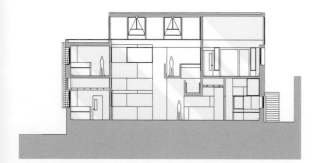

auditorium, offices, meeting rooms, and a foyer space; it also acts as what the architects call "a city-in-miniature." The building is a cauldron that collects public, faculty, and students into its massive foyer space, before directing them into the various private and public areas. This is not an inward-turning or Elyssian fields–type of university building, but rather a vigorous player in the game of the city. A continuous double-height glazed wall pulls users into the building by means of a foyer space at street level. An indication of the main heart of the building, the Aula Magna auditorium, is visible at the corner of the site where the slope of the seating appears in the facade. The substantial foyer for the auditorium is placed by Grafton Architects below street level; indeed a significant portion of the whole building sits underground. Above these areas, transparent bands and skylights filter light and fresh air into the deepest parts of the building. The offices and library in the upper reaches of the building are at once solid pieces of the puzzle but at the same time seem to float above the more public zones of the building. Like the Urban Institute project, the working spaces above allow for cross-disciplinary transfer of ideas and methodologies. In addition to solving complicated programmatic requirements, this project gives the campus an identity center, yet remains a porous framework for the city in which it breathes.

Grafton Architects' project for the Department of Finance, at 7-9 Merrion Row in Dublin, serves many purposes. It is a protected entrance to the complex of government buildings behind with connection to a listed building; it provides office space to a large department; it behaves as a respectful neighbor to a protected Huguenot cemetery; and it acts as significant frontage to one of Dublin's busiest streets, near the city's St. Stephen's Green. This building again questions long-held notions about an assumed solution to a typology, in this case,

"office." Here, workspaces are pulled off the external walls and instead, a timber walkway zone encircles the inner plan. This allows the building a system of natural ventilation; air accepted into the building in the free zone near the windows is drawn into six chimneys dispersed in the plan. In a similar fashion, the main stair of the building is not pushed to a dreary core, but instead weaves the complicated urban environment of Merrion Row into the building. This not only buffers the noise of the street, but acts as a casual meeting space, providing views back across the city with, in some cases, double-height fenestration.

Here, the architects also question the recent trend of offices as throw-away buildings. At Merrion Row, Grafton Architects have determined to express a great solidity of materials. The timber of the main stair is thick and substantial, not flimsy veneer. Likewise, the stone of the facades is not applied as wimpy tiles stuck onto a structural frame, but rather are built in thick blocks; this depth is assuredly exposed at the window reveals and building corners.

The remarkable dexterity with which Grafton Architects completely re-think the standard approach to spatial manipulation runs through the buildings shown here—in the Urban Institute's weaving, in the stacking of programs and design of an animated audience space at Solstice Arts, in the vision of an academic building as a critical part of the city, in the re-alignment of workspaces at 7-9 Merrion Row. Accepted typologies are cross-examined, traditional plans and sections are interrogated. Clearly, Grafton Architects' capacity to reveal new spatial relationships grows out of their propensity for "thick description." They observe not only the epidermal requirements of client, brief, and site, but delve under the skin into the flesh of the question.

Solstice Centre

foyer café

Ros Kavanagh

interior of theater *Hélène Binet*

entrance *Ros Kavanagh*

plan of gallery

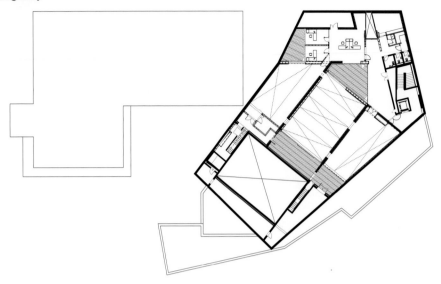

plan of entry level

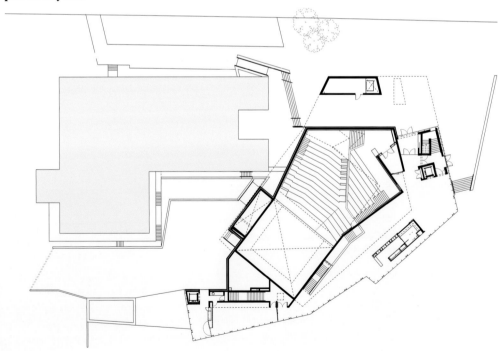

longitudinal section

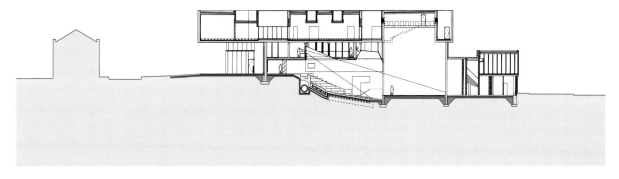

plan of actors' level

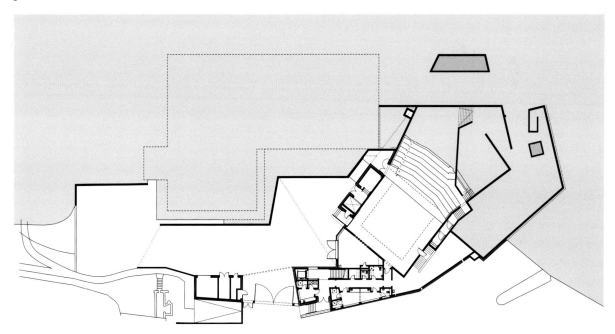

context *Federico Brunetti*

Bocconi University

glazed wall entrance *Grafton Architects*

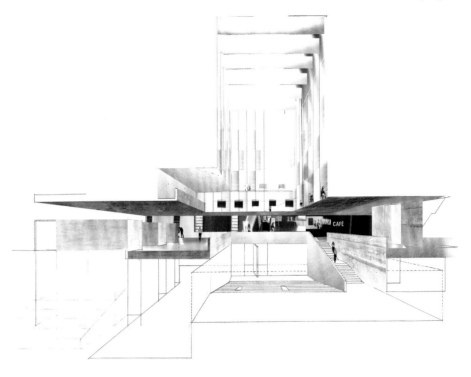

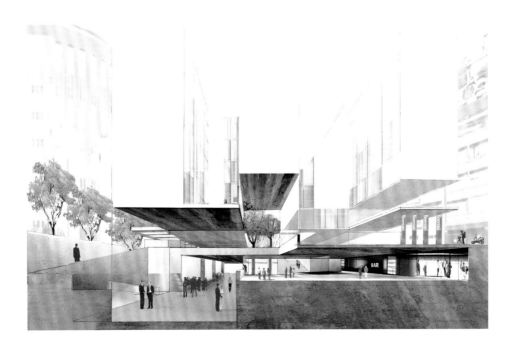

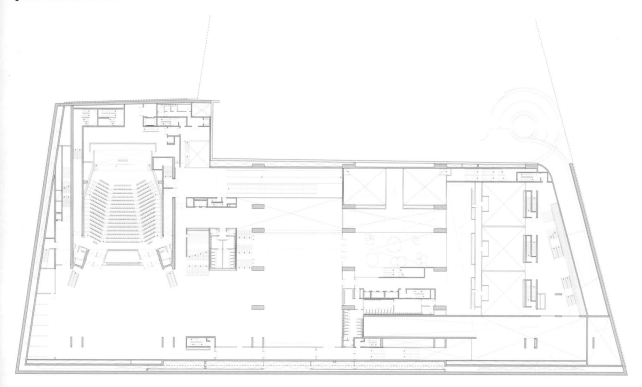

view to offices above
Federico Brunetti

foyer of auditorium
Grafton Architects

stair to lower foyer
Federico Brunetti

Department of Finance

facade to Merrion Row

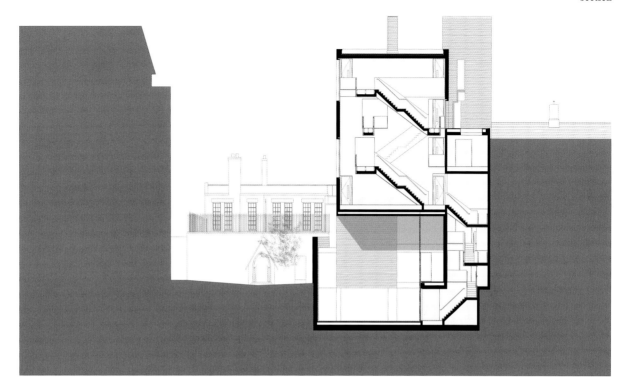

upper floor, first floor, ground floor, and lower ground floor plans

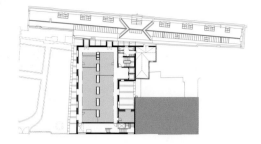

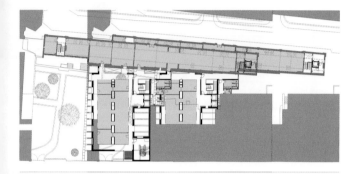

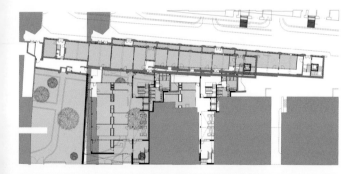

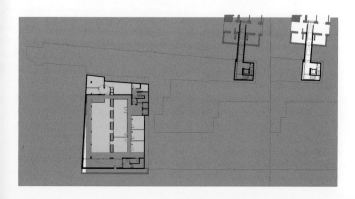

corner

front stair

Dennis Gilbert/VIEW

office space

Donore Youth and Community Centre

Henchion+ Reuter

In *Working Title*, an early text by Martin Henchion and Klaus Reuter, the architect-authors made clear their relationship to their work: "We recognize that Architecture is ultimately beyond words…it is not literature; that it is its own language. Therefore we have tried to distance ourselves from abstract morality and recognize architecture's limits in culture, history and material." For them, architecture is not about connections to philosophy, politics, or art but about a pursuit in its own right, an exploration of space, context, and, in particular, materials. They align themselves with "mainstream" architects, and deliberately so. Theirs is an architecture influenced by the "conversations" they have with projects, their contexts, detailing, and other designers, engineers, and experts.

With the fall of the Berlin Wall, Irish-born Henchion moved to Germany in 1991 and set up an office with Reuter in 1993. They worked together on houses and a series of competitions, winning the design for reconfiguring the Zoological Gardens in Leipzig in 1994, among others. As the anticipated explosion of building projects in the former East Germany failed to materialize and the fierce economic growth in the Republic of Ireland continued to gather speed, Henchion decided to return to Dublin in 1998.

Sustainability for Henchion+Reuter has been part of their work for their entire partnership rather than a recent manifestation of current global anxieties. In this, they view the whole of the building, from its materials to its detailing to its potential programmatic lifespan in its specific community. Much of the duo's Irish work in recent years has focused on community buildings; knowing that the users of the building would almost certainly change over time, perhaps through many iterations, these projects were designed specifically to enable the loosest fit for the greatest number of permutations. Henchion+Reuter also discuss sustainability in the specific language of architecture, in care and innovation taken in detailing. Their views on sustainability also go beyond the limits of buildings: their contribution to the 2006 Venice Biennale examined the possibility of linking areas of Ireland through high-speed train networks.

Commentators often ascribe the Irish buildings by Henchion+Reuter as owing much to an international style. Henchion, however, feels both offices are still in an era of research, still seeking and experimenting with a variety of aesthetic expressions. Henchion spent many of his formative years in Germany and still maintains creative links to the office in Berlin. This certainly permeates the firm's work in Ireland; not only are design solutions solved by both offices, but technology and specific building techniques used in Germany are often incorporated in their projects in Ireland.

Henchion+Reuter's work in Ireland frequently engages with the difficulty of edge conditions, in areas that are neither spatially nor architecturally defined. These peripheral areas allow them to work on buildings in the round, which they relish and regard as the best architectural challenge. Many of Henchion+Reuter's recent commissions have been designed for the hazy, sprawling city that increasingly surrounds Dublin, both new sites redolent with stereotypical Irish countryside, but more often those in nebulous quasi-suburban areas that have become so common on the island, areas not often associated with critical architecture.

The Donore Youth and Community Centre sits in a lower-income area of Dublin, on what used to be the city's formal boundary but is increasingly being redeveloped to include higher-density apartments and office spaces. For the architects, it was important that the building act as a "big house." Henchion likens the building to Giuseppe Terragni's Casa del Fascia: it possesses a villa-like character while still accommodating nondomestic

functions. It would have been unrealistic, he believes, to have tried to explain the building's full functional use on its exterior.

The program for the building was a difficult one: to accommodate both a community center for the surrounding area and drug rehabilitation facilities. Adding further to the project's challenge was the fact that the building was set between an uninspiring church and tattered 1950s council housing.

Henchion+Reuter determined that their answer to the problem should introduce a new form, rectilinear and inward turning, while including views to the community around it and the Dublin hills beyond. The interior rooftop courtyard allows this simultaneous privacy with outward turning, a space the architects brought to the building not asked for in the client's brief. The programmatic requirements are carefully interwoven, with two entrances for different users, but a startling array of visual connections within the sectional arrangement ensures that this does not feel like two buildings. On the top floor, one can see through four layers, down into the main double-height sports hall, across to the rooftop garden space, and through to the mountains on the far side. Here is a singular and sophisticated spatial solution to the complex brief.

The community scheme at Jobstown has a similar, if not more difficult, role to fulfill. The building not only accommodates a day care center, housing for senior citizens, and a local drug-dependency support group but also acts as an anchor to a difficult corner site in one of Dublin's most disadvantaged areas, Tallaght. The area, home to seventy thousand residents, consists mainly of semi-detached housing scattered throughout a landscape of cul-de-sacs and largely unused desertlike green spaces. Joblessness is high, and basic infrastructure—corner shops, post offices, and meeting spaces for residents—had, until the early 2000s, been in short supply.

interior of gym

roof terrace

views through section

Paul Tierney

plan of ground floor

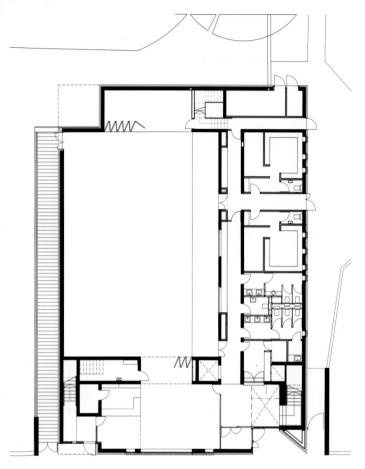

plan of first floor

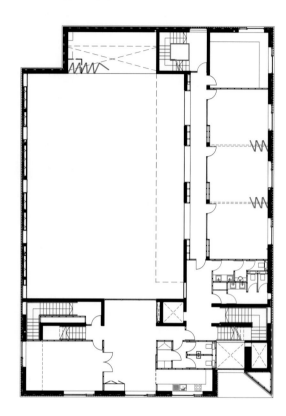

sections

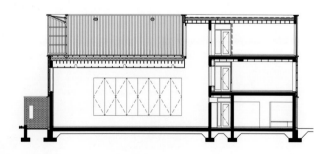

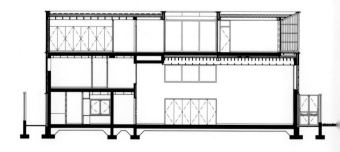

The Henchion+Reuter building is planted on its site in order to produce a corner in anticipation of future development while providing a much-needed service to the vulnerable in the surrounding community. Like Donore Hall, the Jobstown building introduces a timber-lined interior courtyard for children in the day-care center, and covered, inhabitable terraces for the senior residents as antidotes to the building's defensive brick exterior. And like Donore Hall, the building offered Henchion+Reuter the opportunity to work on a building "in the round." Here is the "organize and wrap" concept the architects employ in other schemes in both Germany and Ireland; in part a tectonic strategy, as well as, in this specific site, a method of coping with both the tough environment and the vulnerability of some of the building's users. The wrapping also includes the disparate programmatic requirements: the elements of drug clinic, crèche, and senior housing are kept together in the single building envelope.

Henchion+Reuters's scheme for the Aparthotel, in Kilternan, likewise is forced to engage in edge conditions, though this time, in greatly divergent circumstances. In this project, the building sits in a redevelopment of a hotel and country club, and will provide mid- to high-end housing and hotel accommodation. The challenge here is to incorporate a complex building in a highly sloping and sensitive landscape as part of a larger scheme with other architects. Soon to be connected to the Dublin area's light rail system, this site again sits on the periphery of the city, demanding questions of the nature of a building in such a stereotypically "Oirish" landscape; though this landscape is traditionally more aesthetically "pleasing," the periphery here is no less challenging. The architects begin to answer these issues with careful planning to incorporate specific views to the countryside, roof gardens, and timber cladding in addition to the careful sectional relationship to the site.

After completing the pedestrian bridge in Laufen, Germany, Henchion+Reuter entered and won a competition for a similar project over the Liffey River in Dublin. The new bridge will connect communities of Dublin that, until recently, had poor access to the city's key green space, Phoenix Park. Like Central Park in New York, Phoenix Park acts as an essential "lung" for Dublin, and this project attempts to ensure connection for its adjacent users. Henchion+Reuter's experience in Laufen taught them that ground and preparation works to accept the structure of the bridge should be kept to a minimum to reduce both time and costs. To that end, and to achieve the necessary head height over the water for small boat traffic, their winning entry uses a hollow steel section in what the architects call a "double curved sickle shape," which will be fabricated in a single piece. In the Liffey Bridge project, Henchion+Reuter exhibit a continuation of their understanding of materials and structure, solving the design problem through a direct application of their understanding of how the thing will be made.

The bridge, like all of Henchion+Reuter's schemes, tackles the construction of the problem head-on. Rather than design with construction solutions tacked on at the end of the process, the firm addresses structure and detailing at the inception of projects. It is no surprise that this interest in construction coincides with an ability to interrogate the possibilities of section. What these projects illustrate, too, is Henchion+Reuter's desire to work in contexts without content, in Steven Holl's much-discussed edge conditions. The firm works as well in vast areas of suburban wasteland as in green parkland redolent with atmosphere, but with little built context with which to engage. These spaces with no place are common throughout the island, and Henchion+Reuter is one of the firms bold enough to engage in areas with little or no graspable identity.

Jobstown Centre

corner view of entry

Paul Tierney

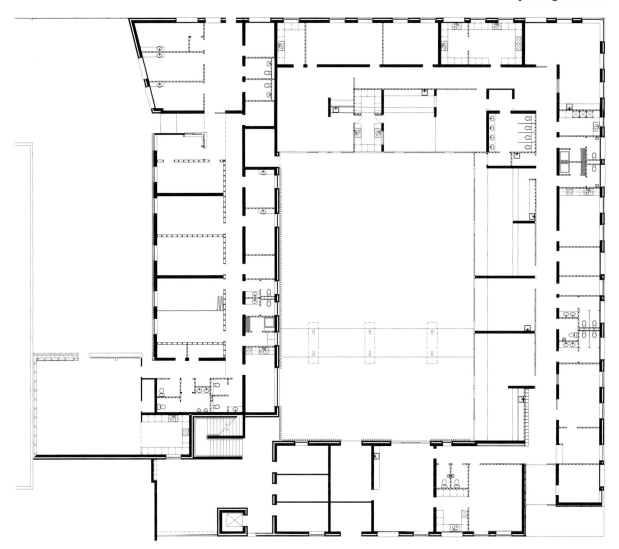

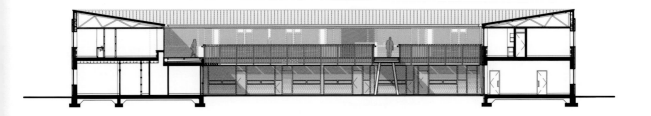

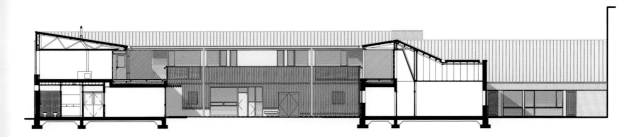

Paul Tierney

Aparthotel Kilternan

upper facade

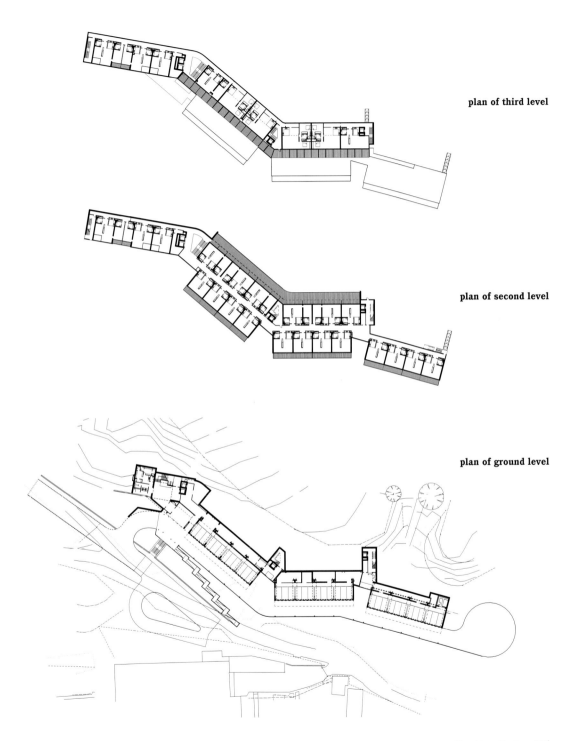

plan of third level

plan of second level

plan of ground level

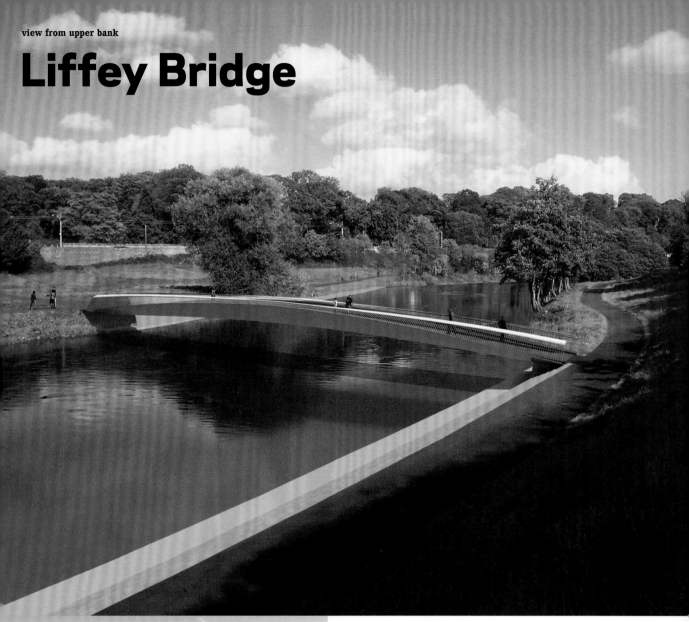

Liffey Bridge

detail view

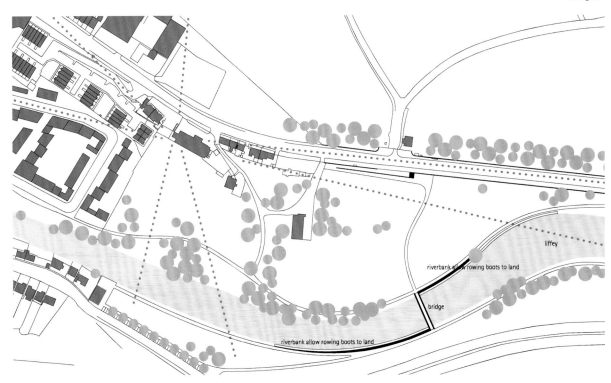

riverbank allow rowing boots to land

liffey

bridge

riverbank allow rowing boots to land

elevation, section, and plan

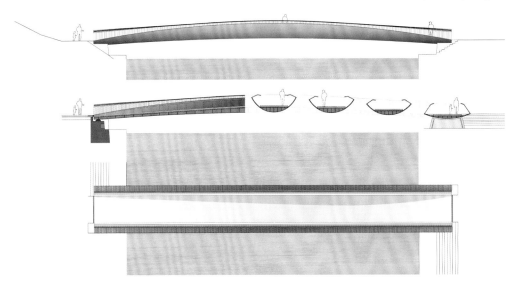

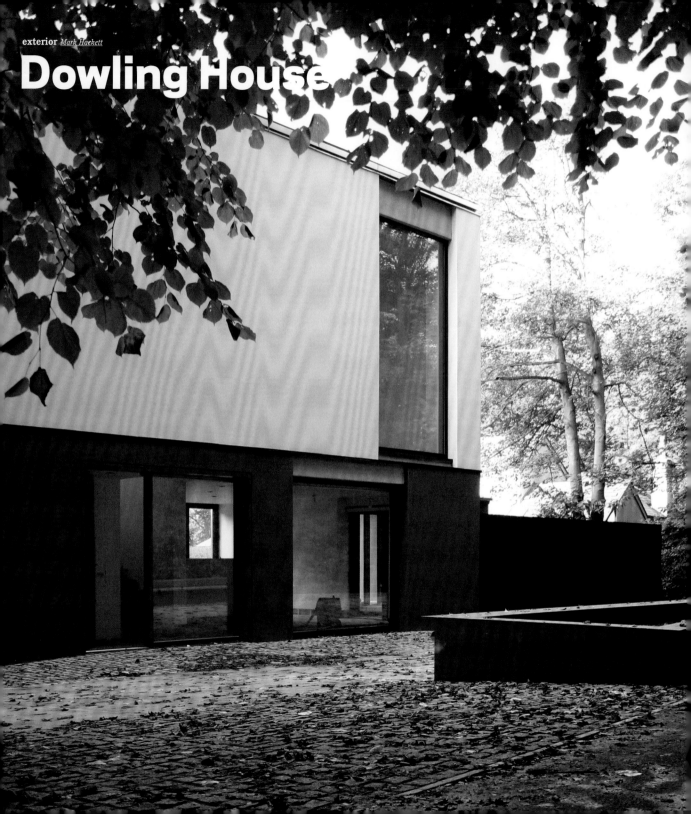

Dowling House

Hackett Hall McKnight

Hackett Hall McKnight considers itself a young practice that deliberates on the nature of architecture for Northern Ireland while maintaining connections to discussions further afield. These connections and conversations are key to the work of Hackett Hall McKnight, as it is committed to a critical, discursive practice. At the same time, its work is imbued with design fluency. A napkin and fountain pen are always close at hand; the architects express ideas not only verbally through teaching and engagement with debate but also in sketch about details, buildings, and the larger urban fabric.

Hackett Hall McKnight states that it is driven not by its aims but by the construction process as whole, including the specific facility and skills of the local construction industry. Álvaro Siza Vieira's influence resonates throughout their practice; as Siza Vieira is comfortable, even keen, to embrace the uncertain, so too is this firm in its approach to architecture. It does not enter into a project with a clear, unassailable vision but questions moves over its entire breadth.

The Dowling House, in a leafy suburb near Belfast, is a building whose simplicity belies several levels of sophisticated moves. The architects view the building as a "thick wall"; this allows for family life to occur within, but maintains a flow around and through the site. Bedrooms in the house's western zone are contrasted with a salon on the first floor that includes a double-height window. Despite the three stories necessary, the elevational treatment of fenestration and lintel pattern, dark base and strong gutter line on a low pitch roof, humanizes its large scale. The house, which clearly follows the villa in a park tradition, embodies calm and modesty rather than bombast.

The MAC, a new building for the Old Museum Arts Centre, is a "different discussion" from the Dowling House. Because the site is wrapped by a new shopping

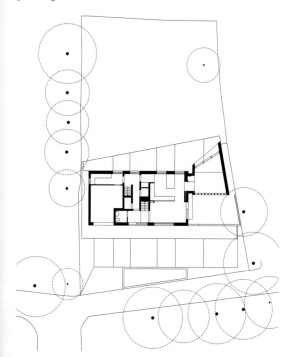

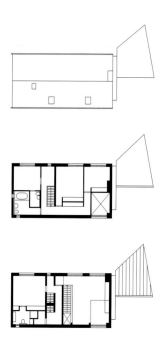

and apartment complex, this major cultural building will have no demonstrative character to the street. Instead, its two major elevations will face a courtyard. Thus the firm's first major commission is, effectively, an interior project—one that inhabits an internal urban space. The building, organized as three blocks of accommodation through careful sectional interaction in its narrow site, combines theater and gallery spaces. The building is suffused with brick, one of Belfast's main building materials; the architects purposefully engage with the material as a recognition of the "tough and robust brick buildings of Victorian Belfast."

For Hackett Hall McKnight, it is "important to create buildings that respond to particular conditions and contribute to a continuity of place." Architecture must be responsive to the material and formal traditions of construction common to Northern Ireland's cities and countryside. Hackett Hall McKnight designs buildings

that are at once significant and confidently modest; theirs is an architecture that will contribute to the debate about the future and quality of Northern Ireland's built environment.

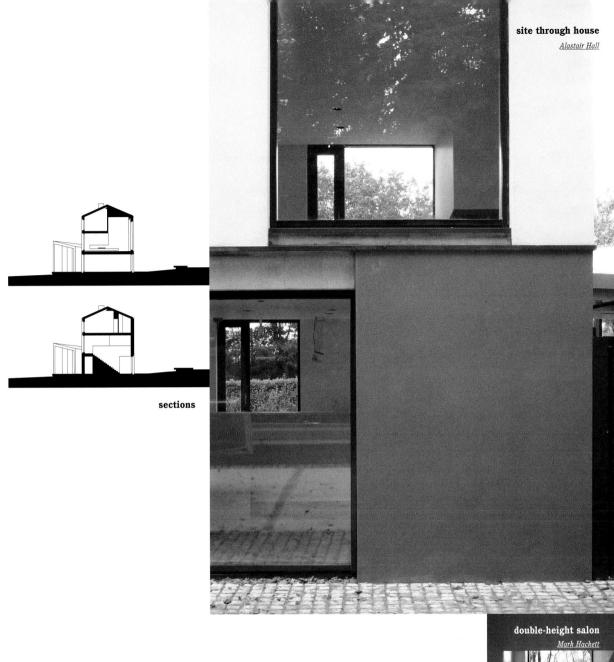

site through house
Alastair Hall

sections

double-height salon
Mark Hackett

MAC

view with cathedral

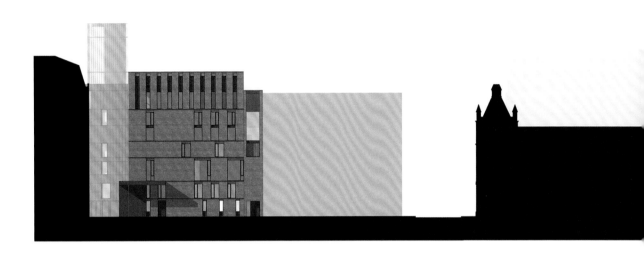

view of courtyard

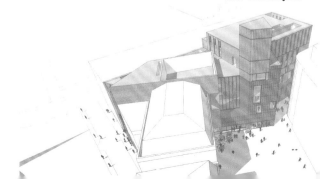

plan of fourth floor

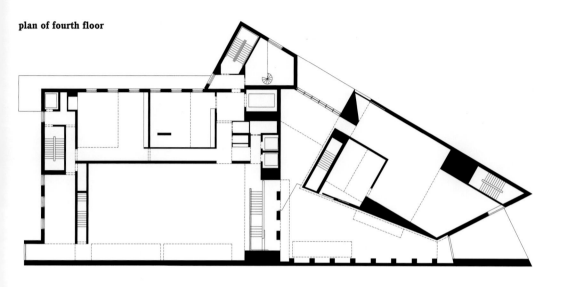

plan of first floor

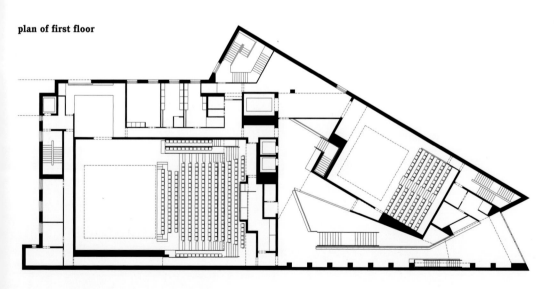

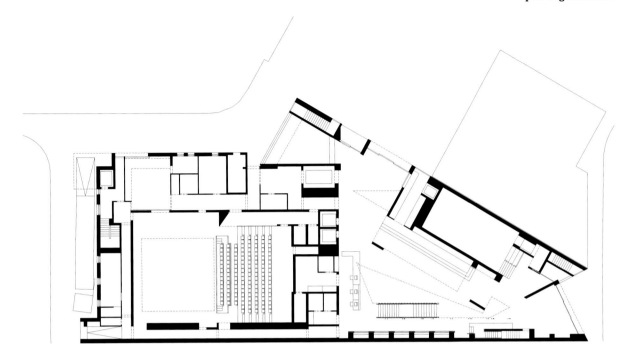

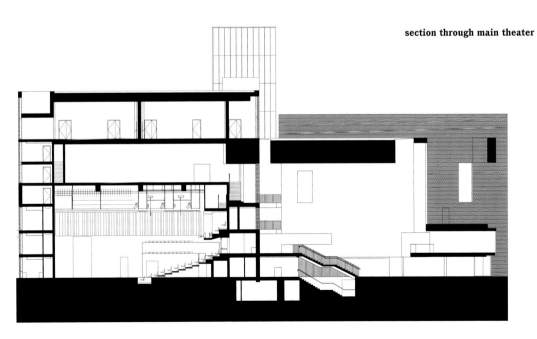

Aras Chill Dara

heneghan.peng
.architects

As winners of some of the most significant architectural competitions in the last ten years, heneghan.peng .architects has rapidly become one of Ireland's most high-profile practices. Like Bucholz McEvoy, the partnership of Róisín Heneghan and Shih-Fu Peng is transatlantic. They studied together at Harvard, then worked in New York City on competitions in their "spare" time while carrying out day jobs for Skidmore, Owings & Merrill and Michael Graves. They too moved to Dublin after winning the competition for a new county council headquarters, in their case, for County Kildare in 2000. In 2003, they won one of the largest architectural competitions ever, the Grand Egyptian Museum, beating out 1,556 other entries from 83 countries. That same year they won an invited competition for a hotel in Dublin. Taking this in their stride, they then entered the competition for Dublin's Carlisle Pier, which they won in 2004. And if that weren't enough, they then pocketed the most sought-after project in Northern Ireland by winning the competition for the new Visitor Centre for the Giant's Causeway, a World Heritage site, in 2005. Understandably, they are constantly barraged with the question: from whence does this uncanny ability arise? Heneghan answers simply, "We enter many competitions often." They also admit to an ability to quickly analyze and understand site conditions, programmatic requirements, and the clients' essential desires for the building.

Most of their competition-winning entries are gargantuan in scale. Heneghan.peng.architects sees this as an opportunity: the buildings have the ability to affect the fabric around them, whether they are set in harsh natural terrain or in urban environments. They are so large that they will affect and dictate social spaces, the fabric of the built environment, and the infrastructure of public space. Thus, for heneghan.peng.architects, architecture also must include a manipulation of the

157

landscape; they cut, embed, and extend the topographies that surround their buildings, spending as much energy in considering the ground plane as they do the building sitting on, or more often than not, in it. Surprisingly for the scale being handled by the practice, these are bold but simple moves.

The problem heneghan.peng.architects faced at the council offices in Kildare was not an easy one. The new building had to provide spaces for a civil service client in mid-Ireland trying to provide a type of service to citizens never before used. Client and architect were also striving for a deep-seated transparency for the site and in the building's physical form, one that allowed access to a democratic process and the social mechanisms that make up contemporary everyday life.

Aras Chill Dara occupies a prominent site at the edges of a typical small Irish town. For the architects, the landscape surrounding the building was critical to its formation as a democratic mechanism. The park slopes slowly upward to the building, which rises out of the back of the site, setting the building in a literal and metaphorical amphitheater. Recalling Anthony Vidler in *Architecture of the Uncanny*, Peng speaks of the building that for him has no facade, just a "fragmented surface that you move along." This is reflected in the building's translucent sloping skin and the core set of transparent sloping ramps that link one office "bar" to the other. Much lighter and broader than Bernard Tschumi's similar circulation space at Columbia University, the ramps allow members of the public to ascend to the top floor. Although the actual work spaces of the council departments are closed to the public, the height a visitor can reach and the ability to see through the layers of transparent facade allow for startling access to the building. Thus Aras Chill Dara succeeds where other projects built to embody materially the transparency of democracy, like the Welsh Assembly, do not: most of the structure is physically accessible to the public. Rooms are not simply made transparent for visual access; rather the whole building encourages, particularly through the ramp system, an interaction with council members and civil servants—those who make a democracy work.

For the Giant's Causeway Visitor Centre, heneghan .peng.architects knew that it had to fulfill the requirements for the brief but not in any way detract from the site, the most visited area in Northern Ireland and its best-known tourist destination. The new building and necessary parking had to accommodate huge numbers of tourists, introduce them to the scientific and cultural aspects of the geology, and offer respite from the lengthy steep climb required to return from the Causeway itself. The architects assert that this was a building that had to be about landscape first and architecture second.

This is a building that will be inhabited above and below. The existing upper coastal path winds its way through the site by way of a ramp that emerges onto the roof of the new building. To get down to the Causeway stones, one passes through the building and back out into the descent. Heneghan.peng.architects carefully maintained the ridge line of the existing landscape, and the building and car park are thus almost completely imperceptible from the sea side. Ironically, after the amount of political wrangling involved in green-lighting the project, the architecture will be largely invisible in its finished form.

The Grand Egyptian Museum in reality will dwarf even its grandiose title. It will contain 80,000 sq m/860,000 sq ft of space, including 30,000 sq m/320,000 sq ft for exhibitions and a front wall that will stretch a full kilometer/over half a mile. Heneghan.peng.architects wanted their design to address both the pyramid site as well as the close proximity of Cairo, two sites dense with historical and social identities. To make sense of the site's vast and overwhelming political and cultural

building in landscape *Dennis Gilbert/VIEW*

ramp view *Dennis Gilbert/VIEW*

site plan

plan of first floor

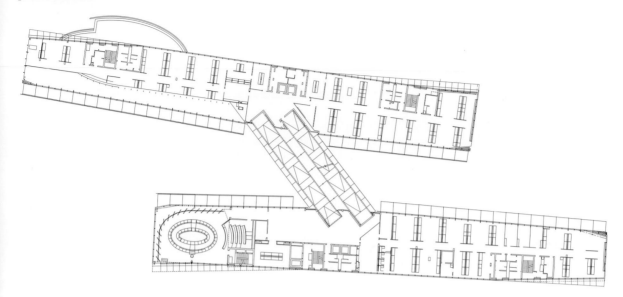

plan of ground floor

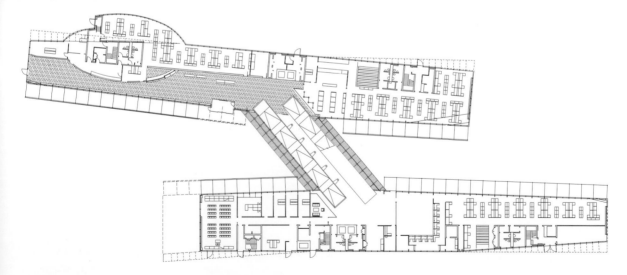

potency, the architects read the desert as inscribed with lines, and the building arises from these seminal cuts in the floodplain, a "series of trajectories and surfaces that one moves through." Much of the plan is generated from lines inscribed by views to either the pyramids or the city.

The building is approached from the city side, by passing from a forecourt through the translucent stone wall into the main entrance area. From there, the museum is organized around a grand stair, which acts not only as a way to move people but as an orienting device to which visitors can refer when moving through the vast space. At various levels in the enormous stairs, one can branch off to areas for special exhibitions, classrooms, and storage of the immense collection. At the far end of the stair is the ultimate view to the Pyramids and the Sphinx, though the main destination of the stair is a series of galleries.

Peng views the museum "more as landscape than building, where the gardens and their relation to the exhibition show the workings and influence of the Nile on the great Egyptian civilization." The building is so large, and on such an accelerated schedule, that they have teamed up with the Advanced Geometry Unit of the structural engineering firm Ove Arup to help devise formulas for their grid and dimensioning systems. They have decided, too, that the technology required to run a collection and building of this scale should become a major architectural element; the walls in which the digital technology is based also act as dividers between the various exhibition galleries. Here, then, is a seemingly impossible collapse of scales: heneghan.peng .architects not only use the immense landscape, city, and enormous monuments to inform the building but also fingertip elements of a far smaller scale, which will ultimately affect individuals at a minute level.

One must wonder how heneghan.peng.architects' work would have developed had it not won a series of enormous buildings requiring extremely sensitive responses to site. The architects do not seem interested in glorifying their projects as signature buildings. Rather, they emphasize "the importance of inhabitation, use and performance of a building." This indicates a refreshing modesty on their part; it is also a consequence of their intelligent response, from the foundation of the firm as young architects to issues as problematic as access to democracy, fragile natural environments, and possibly the world's most important archaeological site. Heneghan .peng.architects has determined that for every project, its architecture must be as much landscape as building, in terms of both scale and the impact it will make on the events that will occur within, on, and among it.

Giant's Causeway Visitor Centre

roof extending into landscape

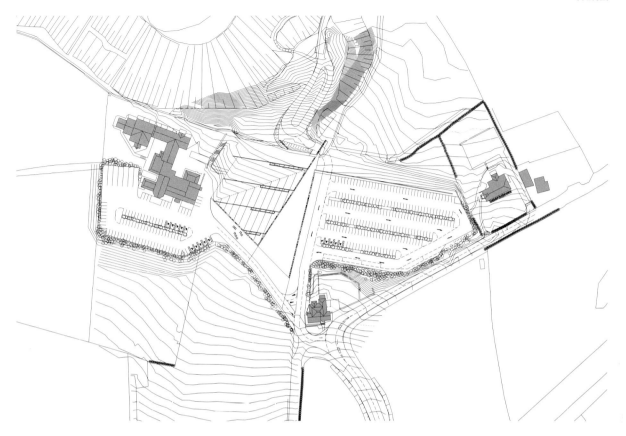

site plan

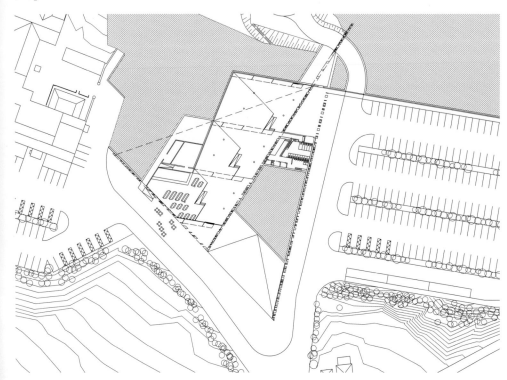

elevation and section

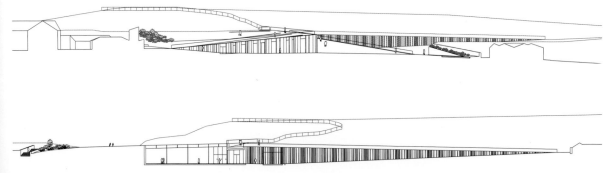

view from Causeway

view from railway station

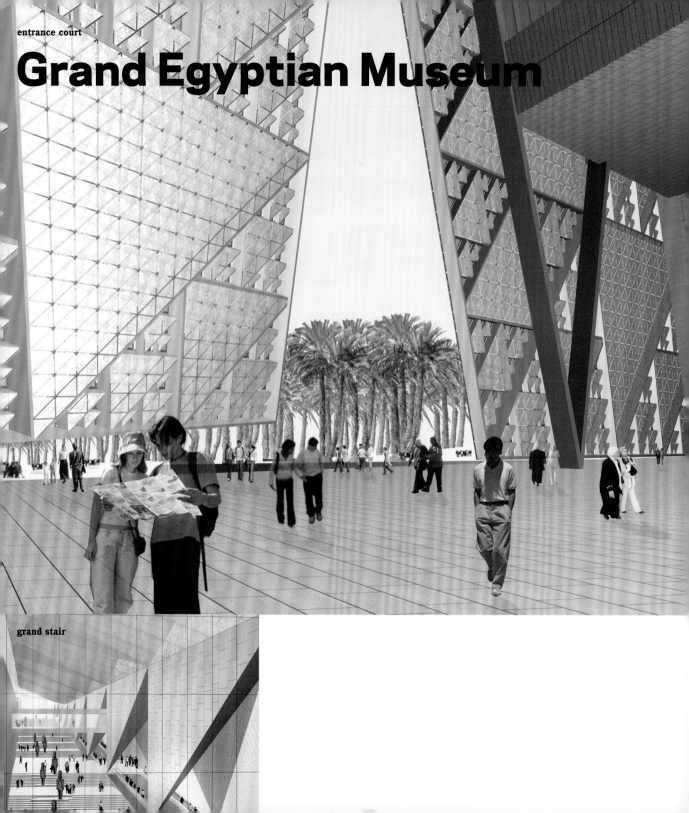

entrance court

Grand Egyptian Museum

grand stair

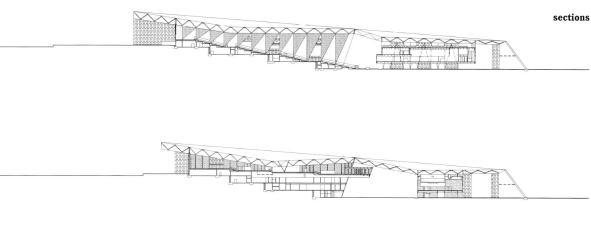

entrance level and gallery level plans

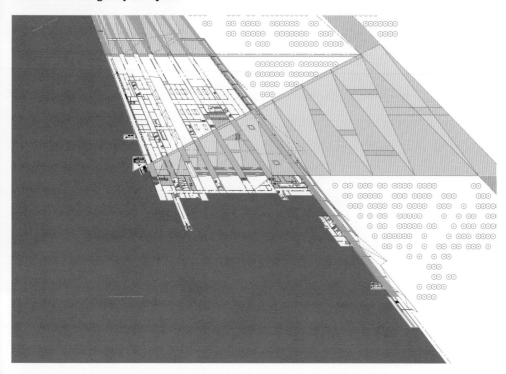

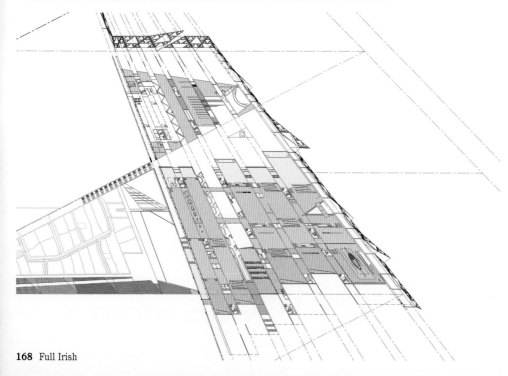

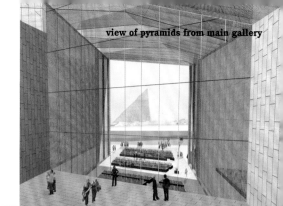
view of pyramids from main gallery

translucent stone facade

view to grand stair from entrance court

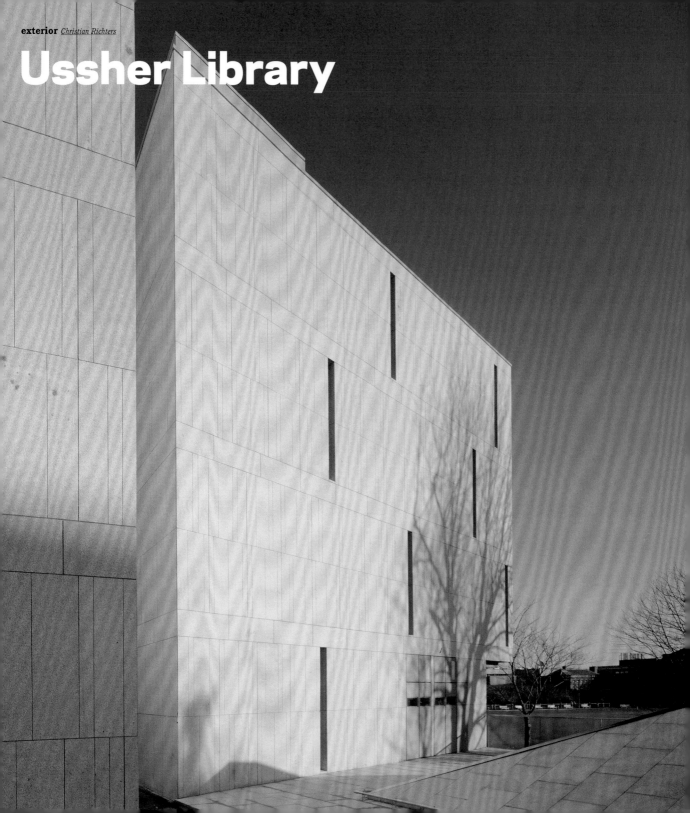

Ussher Library

McCullough Mulvin Architects

To understand the way Niall McCullough and Valerie Mulvin work is to understand how they spent their time in the doldrums that were the 1980s and early 1990s in Dublin. This was not a period that McCullough Mulvin spent sitting on their hands bewailing their lot; instead they combed the countryside in search of "the nature of architecture in Ireland." They produced two books: *A Lost Tradition,* jointly, and *Palimpsest: Change in the Irish Building Tradition,* authored by McCullough alone, which examined, in turn, the typologies found in the Irish landscape and the changes that had been wrought in native building traditions. McCullough also wrote *Dublin: An Urban History*, which similarly investigated the urban form of the country's largest city.

As part of Group 91, which transformed Temple Bar and decidedly created a voice for contemporary Irish architecture, McCullough Mulvin began to design buildings that are purposefully and inextricably linked to the historical and physical environments in which they sit. It is no accident that most of their work inhabits tough, irregular, often contentious places. They delve into the question of how a new building can write itself onto the gradations of an Irish city or town. In conversation, McCullough describes a site as "a kind of archaeological landscape which requires time before you can sense the traces of other orders, earlier layers upon it." Site for McCullough Mulvin seems to be more than simply a surface on which new architecture is built; site becomes as potent as if it were a building itself.

The Ussher Library, at Trinity College, Dublin, is an excellent example of this involvement in existing sites with all the formal and cultural layers that can be embedded in them. The extension, won through competition with the Dublin firm KMD, was not a project for a tenuous practice unsure of these issues. It had to provide new accommodation for students, books, and offices, negotiate a cramped inner-city site with high visibility from all sides, and still exert enough of an individual identity to act as sibling to one of Dublin's best-loved modernist buildings from the 1960s, ABK's Berkeley Library.

McCullough Mulvin determined a simple design concept to solve this tricky architectural problem: three blocks, each with its own formal character, on a podium. While still adhering to the Trinity grid, the new blocks reorient their users' views through atria, rooflights, and long views across internal spaces. The difficult integration of three libraries—the Berkeley, the Lecky, and the Ussher itself—is orchestrated in a roundhouse under the plinth that creates an addition to the numerous Trinity courtyards above. The reading spaces are separated by a grand canyon of an atrium, stretching upward eight stories. The reading room facade, which faces the university's cricket ground, alternately reflects the foliage of the existing mature trees, glints with low-angled sun, and gives views into the new reading space filled with students bent over books and laptops. Though the building clearly speaks to the earlier ABK building and is posited by the architects as three sculptural stone blocks on a podium, it is nonetheless far lighter than its 1960s compatriot.

The Waterford City Library had to fit into another tight existing situation, this time in a small southeastern town best known for its crystal factory. The main library was to reinhabit an existing building from 1905, moving upward and outward into space it had not previously occupied. The new limestone facades of the extensions, both to the side and above the existing structure, continue the material of the old building but treat it in a new manner. Clearly these elevations to the town are key aspects of the project, but McCullough Mulvin describe the library as a "closed box, geometry rather than geography." Much of their work on this building is

"secret" to the interior of the existing corner building. The architects combined the remaining old structure of double-height brick arches and pillars with in-situ concrete and walnut-lined walls, bookcases, seating, desks, and stairwells. Unlike of the idea of the traditional library—a place of sedentary study and internal reflection—the building is one in which movement is key to its use and enjoyment. Walking through the reading spaces, research areas, audio listening stations, and meeting rooms, new views constantly emerging through windows and openings that seem to serve a dual purpose of lighting a deep plan and adding to the understanding of the building within the city, even expanding the very typology of "library" as an institution of additive layers.

The Virus Reference Laboratory Extension, University College, Dublin, had to cope with a wholly different set of site and programmatic issues. UCD's Bellfield campus was masterplanned with buildings set as individual objects in a large suburban-rural context to the southeast of Dublin's city center. As the university has burgeoned, additional buildings must play a role "to ask the masterplan if it's still appropriate," in the words of McCullough Mulvin. The brief, somewhat overwhelmingly, also called for the proper expression in such a bucolic setting for a building filled with some of the most deadly organisms on earth. The addition addresses these issues with its external envelope, in the language of a timber-clad pavilion, which seems to meld with the existing landscape. As the timber has aged, the building quietly recedes into its semirural environment, but the reflections from its large panes of glass recall its purpose as a serious, inhabitable research space.

Thurles is what might be classed as a "typical" Irish town, with a car-filled main square bounded by two- and three-story terraced houses and shops, a river, a tiny train station, and the ubiquitous suburban housing developments growing in increasing numbers on what

library facade

three blocks on a plinth

Christian Richters

atrium

plan of podium level

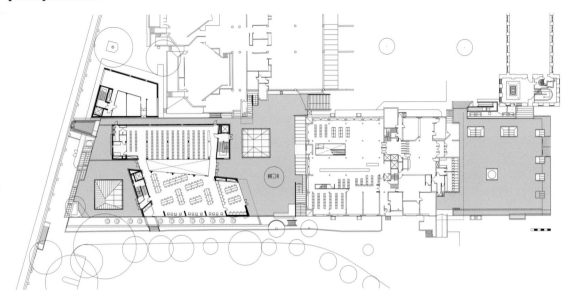

long section

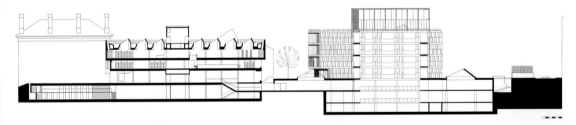

elevation to cricket ground

were formerly the outskirts of the town. McCullough Mulvin's Source Arts Centre and Library, set in one of Thurles's most prominent positions, adjacent to the main bridge of the town, is thus all the more surprising given the convention of the surroundings. Many other arts centers in Ireland have been used as cultural regeneration projects, but the Source is instead an assembly of programs, a universal space for a myriad of cultural events, displays, workshops, and performances for a wide audience.

For the architects, the Centre is "intensely about geography." In contrast to the interior world of Waterford, this project centers on notions of the town fabric being asked to become a building. Ruth O'Herlihy, the third director in the practice, states that Thurles is a conscious development from the Ussher project—a podium with elements, again in a tripartite system, this time with specific reference to the river as its main site influence. They describe it as an "underground building that's above ground, with its roots exposed."

At the pedestrian entrance level, the building is surrounded by new public spaces, terraces that overlook the river and the town. The ground seems to rise up and over the building, creating walls that merge into the roof and back down into the plinth on the other side, while the longer side walls show their sectional cut with full-height glazing. The building's interior continues to emit an alternative way to inhabit a small town, with a double-height library using the timber-clad poured concrete seen at Waterford and pinpoints of eager orange stairs and beams. While the library is the busiest, perhaps most public part of the building, McCullough Mulvin also designed a cavernous, top-lit gallery space hidden behind an enormous sliding timber door at the building's entrance. The final component of the building, the 250-seat auditorium, spills out into a bar and external timber terrace. As extraordinary as the form of the building is to the traditional surroundings, it does indeed emit a geographic presence, embedded both physically and socially in the fabric and use of the town and its hinterlands.

The early research of McCullough and Mulvin as young architects has proved a seminal event for their later careers. These books may have been written with an eye to future work or made in and for themselves as documents for their personal understanding of the built environment of Ireland at the time. Whatever the original motive, their practice has clearly derived much of its skill and facility from this early work. They are most at home in the difficult strata of sites that have been built and overbuilt. It is a practice gripped with the change of buildings and how these changes affect an entire landscape.

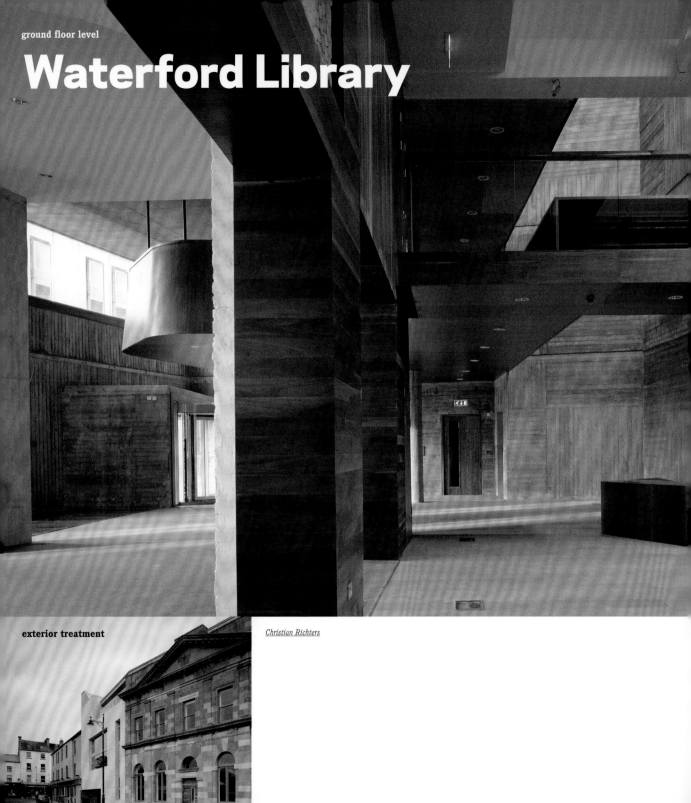

Waterford Library

exterior treatment

Christian Richters

site location

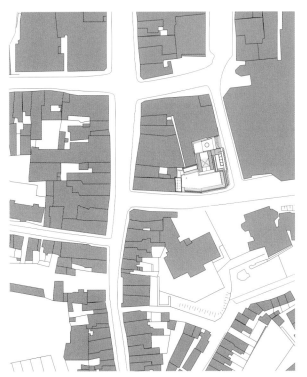

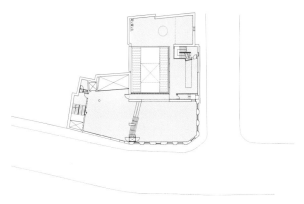

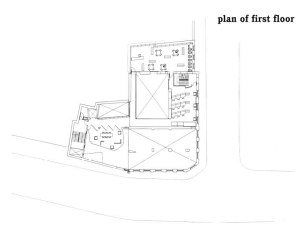

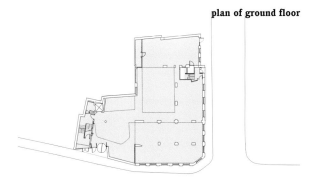

McCullough Mulvin Architects **177**

section

ground floor reading area *McCullough Mulvin Architects*

stair

reading area

UCD Virus Ref Lab

Christian Richters

link

context

location

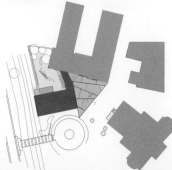

plan of ground floor

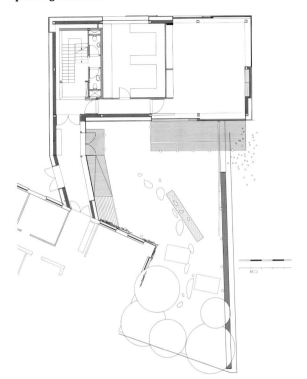

plan of first floor

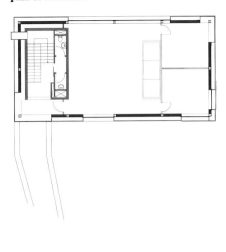

section through labs

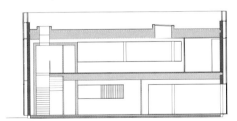

section showing link

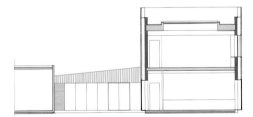

McCullough Mulvin Architects **181**

Source Arts Centre and Library

facade to deck

Christian Richters

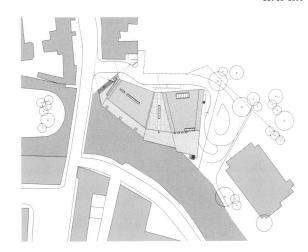

plan of ground floor

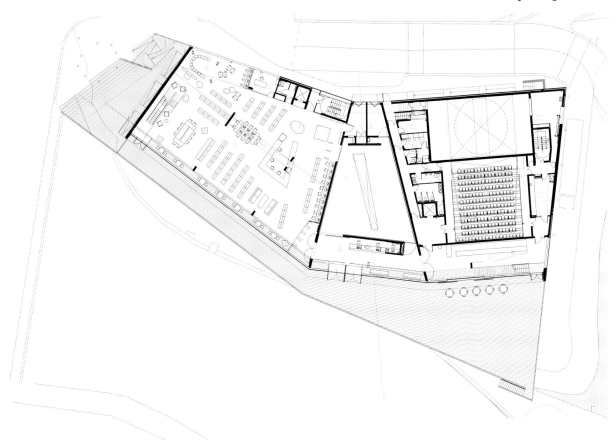

front elevation

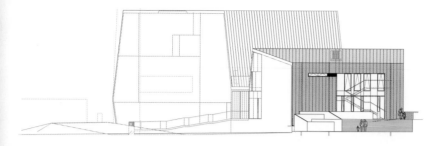

long section

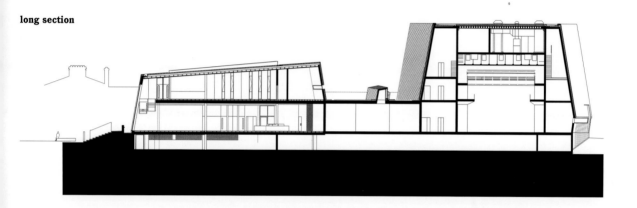

library

main stair of library

Christian Richters

reflection of town

Brookfield Community and Youth Centre

Hassett Ducatez Architects

Gráinne Hassett describes her firm's approach to design as twofold. First, it "tries to ascertain what the place and the people need, rather than making an architectural piece that is self-referential." She sees this as a means of being "strategic" in response to practice based in urban considerations. Second, Hassett Ducatez investigates the visual, "how things seem and look." This latter approach entails careful consideration of material and color and its deployment in external and internal applications. It is in the conflation of these two approaches where the firm's work resonates, where the solution to particular programmatic requirements meets research into visual awareness.

Hassett learned much of her craft, like so many Irish architects, on extensions to inner-city homes. The very small scale of projects afforded the firm the opportunity to concentrate on minute details and to experiment with ideas in built form. Like Dominic Stevens, Hassett was awarded the Arts Council of Ireland's Kevin Kieran Award to carry out architectural research for two years. Hassett spent the time exploring visual perception of the built environment and the role, condition, and prejudices of the contemporary viewer.

The Glass House represents an opportunity for the firm to explore this research within the context of an extension and freestanding house for one extended family. The project experiments with different types of glass in order to exploit what Colin Rowe defined as "the evasive nature" of transparency, examining both issues of privacy and the collapse of interior/exterior.

As the scope of work for the firm has increased, so too has the exploration of larger urban design work, particularly at the behest of local authorities. The firm's plans for new developments attempt to anticipate different uses for space designed in a single, flexible overarching plan, whether the areas are used for housing, offices, public open spaces, parking, or industry.

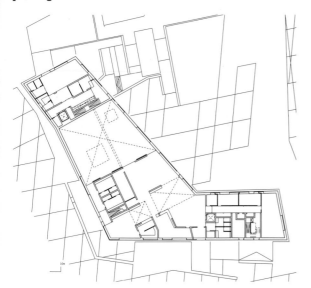

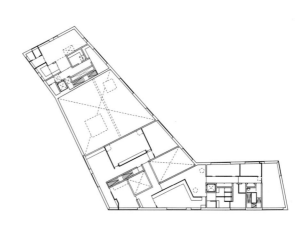

The Brookfield Community and Youth Centre represents a considerable excursion into the suburban sprawl of Dublin. It is a difficult environment in which to work; a limited context offers little reference, and few elements in the built environment give clues about an appropriate architectural response. This is the same area of Dublin in which Henchion+Reuter's Jobstown Centre sits, a region that is desertlike in both built and social terms; there are few locations for community gatherings and minimal shared infrastructure. The new building faces the challenge of giving the area a "quality" of instilling some "there" there while providing a building accessible to the community. At Brookfield, the firm's interest in the visual is manifest in the configuration of the facade and in the use of varying colors throughout the building embedded into its fabric. The floor is poured orange resin, the doors are veneered in tough-wearing laminate in various colors, and the exterior panels vary in hue and material as they reach around the building. In this landscape, this startling building deploys a strong statement: that community matters, that buildings, even those based in a substantially theoretical framework, can make an enormous difference to the contexts in which they are built.

Hassett Ducatez's work arises from research in the most compelling way for an architect, allowing abstract notions to be tested in both text and in buildings. This is a fundamentally critical practice, one that has created at Brookfield a building that itself requires a reflective response about issues far wider than accommodation or construction. This building—and, one imagines, future buildings by Hassett Ducatez—not only solves the complex problem posed by the site, small budget, and program but asks in turn that questions about the quality of the built environment be considered by its viewers.

courtyard/playspace *Ros Kavanagh*

section

foyer and games space *Michael Duffy*

Glass House

corner detail

Ros Kavanagh

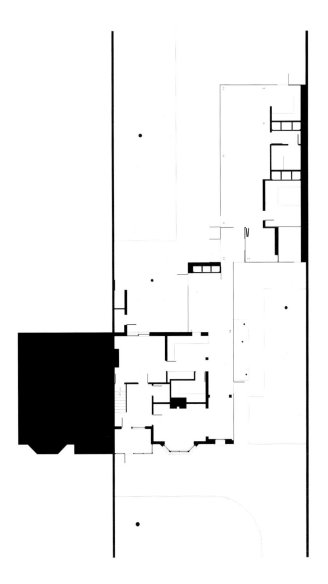

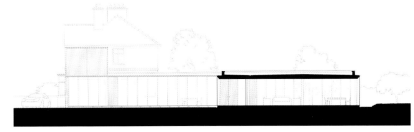

Letterkenny Public Services Centre

MacGabhann Architects

In 1997, Tarla and Antoin MacGabhann returned home to Letterkenny, a town in County Donegal in the northwest of Ireland, to carry on the practice started by their father in 1975. Antoin, a civil engineer, and Tarla, an architect, had spent years away—Antoin in Glasgow and London, and Tarla in Berlin, where he worked on the Jewish Museum by Daniel Liebeskind. Letterkenny is a strange town to which to return: once a small village, it has since exploded in a riot of new development, seemingly unconstrained, unplanned, even unwanted. The MacGabhanns are working in a real edge city, a smaller but by no means less bewildering set of circumstances that faces the former small villages that surround Dublin.

Working in Donegal has many peculiarities. Outside the Belfast and Dublin architectural milieus, the MacGabhanns often work in isolation, which, they acknowledge, "has good and bad points." The geopolitical context on the island locates Donegal simultaneously in the Republic of Ircland and in Ulster; perhaps more than any other county, Donegal is connected to both north and south. There is little spectacular architecture to which to respond, materially or spatially; architecture in Donegal must consider a modest response first when situating itself in this particular rural landscape. Because Donegal is located at the top left corner of Ireland, architects here often find themselves trying to balance and sometimes sacrifice the dual issues of views (normally to the north) and sunlight (from the south). The views, too, are difficult to prioritize; Donegal commands aspects out to sea and across tracts of heather-covered mountains in multiple directions. There also exists the omnipresent power of Liam McCormick, perhaps Ireland's greatest twentieth-century architect. His importance, which is always in the background, must be met, challenged, used, or abandoned.

The MacGabhanns spend a great deal of energy on the control of geometry. "There is always an overriding rule keeping the geometry in check," they explain. There may be a subsidiary system, or even a tertiary one, but all moves, all lines are drawn according to rules. Having learned to manipulate complex forms on a drawing board in the early 1990s, before computerized technology came to its current level of sophistication, MacGabhann Architects won't allow its work to get unruly. The choice of a minimal palette of materials, too, helps "keep the buildings calm"; initial investigations of multiple types of concrete aggregate, metals, and paint colors are edited down to tie the designs back to a simplicity that corresponds to the Donegal landscape.

The Letterkenny Public Services Centre is another of the Republic of Ireland's civic buildings that provides services to local residents as well as a focal point for local council meetings. Its site on the edge of the sprawl of Letterkenny looks across a field to the spire of the town's main church. However, MacGabhann Architects was conscious that this field would not exist for long—new urban/suburban development would soon rise in conversation with their new civic building.

This building itself prioritizes the journey for those who visit and use it. The main approach is a road that branches off Letterkenny's main street before it reaches the town center, thus instilling a feeling of detachment from the original townscape. In the car park, the approach meets the road with rough-pour concrete. The slowly ramping ground plane continues into the building and proceeds into the concrete and timber-filled public areas, most of which can be seen from the front door. The ramp that began in the car park rises to the council chamber with its large window overlooking both the route of arrival and the church on the other side of the town. The ramp then continues back into the building before culminating on the sebum roof.

The Regional Cultural Centre in Letterkenny is meant to serve both performing and visual arts. Its site, off the town's main street, faces back toward the main southern approach. It connects, too, to the space behind, with a pedestrian link to the quieter northern side of Letterkenny. The building is planned around a pedestrian sequence that progresses up the slope of the site. The route enters the building at the main entrance marked by yellow-gold panels and leads through and across the building, terminating at a window that overlooks Letterkenny in the main gallery space. The stairs escalate across the front facade of the building, and each landing allows a visual or spatial connection across the standing seam roof.

This passage is a journey through a single landscape that follows on from similar gestures at the Council Offices. With these two buildings, MacGabhann Architects seem to be making a statement about the nature of civic projects: the journeys through the buildings allow visitors to examine the quasi-urban area where they sit, both the traditional street pattern of the original town and the sprawl that continues to grow on its outskirts.

Tuath na Mara sits on the banks of Lough Swilly, one of Ireland's largest sea inlets. The traditional Donegal rural house, based on a typically 17.5-foot/5.3-meter plan, sandwiched a living space between bedrooms at either end; Tuath na Mara is based on this tradition. MacGabhann Architects thinks of this house as a container made site specific by its views. The house was designed for a couple who often have friends or colleagues staying with them, sometimes for extended periods. To that end, the building was designed to be two houses—"pair of semi-detached houses back to back." The house is entered at a midpoint; one then continues right or left along a library-clad corridor. Within the library panels are doors that, when opened perpendicular

entry facade

sebum roof

interior of first floor

Dennis Gilbert/VIEW

plan of ground floor

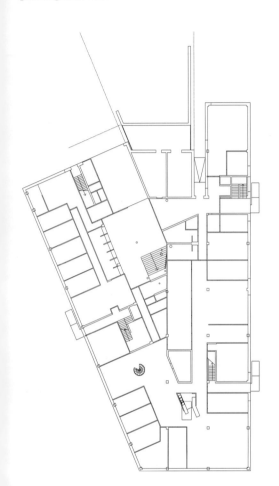

plan of first floor

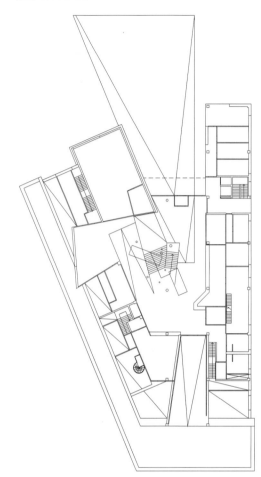

section

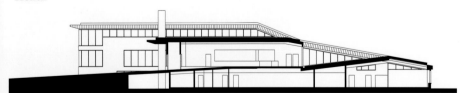

196 Full Irish

to the walls, can close off one end of the house from the other for total privacy. The library corridor is illuminated with slices of light brought in from incisions in both roof and wall.

To one side of the front door is a smaller guesthouse, with sleeping, bath, and living spaces; to the other is the larger main house, with kitchen and more significant living space. Both end rooms have been specially tailored to attune themselves to the views and light, the ceilings flicking up to make the best use of the sun. Because the house is approached from above by a steep winding road, the architects carefully considered the fifth facade, the roof. It is here that the MacGabhanns' interest in manipulating geometry is exhibited despite the project's small size. They chose and then sourced pre-patinated, black zinc standing-seam cladding for both roof and walls—a material that disappears into the landscape, especially when viewed from the lower beach or from the water. The material harks back to technology of the ubiquitous holiday caravan, shipping containers, temporary buildings that sit lightly on the landscape.

Teach Annie has a history with the MacGabhanns: the client's original house on the site was remodeled and extended by their father; when the clients wanted to build a new house, they contacted his sons. The new house reflects MacGabhann Architects' continuing interest in manipulating geometries and committing to a "responsibility to attuning to the surrounding buildings." The white plasterwork external finish and large pitch, dark, corrugated fiber cement roof reflect the modest local building materials. The building is cut into an existing berm, setting it farther into the landscape and carefully orchestrating views out to sea and back across the Donegal Mountains. Thick walls, also characteristic of local building traditions, are punctured by windows with mill-finished, untreated aluminum reveals that extend 4 inches/100 mm from the plane of the wall.

These windows are frames—holes punched in the walls rather than floor-to-ceiling walls of glass. "It's the way architecture in Donegal is made," according to the architects. The open-plan living and kitchen space is punctuated with a Douglas fir–lined fireplace area. This journey to the fireplace at the far end of the room is then taken up into the roof space, into a timber-framed aerie that overlooks the stunning views the site affords.

Most commentators of MacGabhann Architects' work reflect on the influence of Berlin, particularly in the manipulation of geometry and use of metal cladding from the Jewish Museum and the Berlin Philharmonic. Perhaps more interesting is a clear affinity for instilling buildings with a journey that Hans Scharoun, in particular, commands in the Philharmonic and State Library. MacGabhann Architects' buildings, whether civic or domestic, contain spatial events that are continuations of the movement of the building outside the external fabric and into the surrounding landscape. Grand stairs continue onto roofs, floors extend into the landscape to afford dramatic views, public spaces flow into private ones. The path is used not only programmatically in their buildings but to reflect on the natural landscape and development of Donegal as a whole, on the history and future of the region in which the buildings and these architects are so embedded.

Regional Cultural Centre Letterkenny

facade in hill context

Dennis Gilbert/VIEW

plans of ground floor and first floor

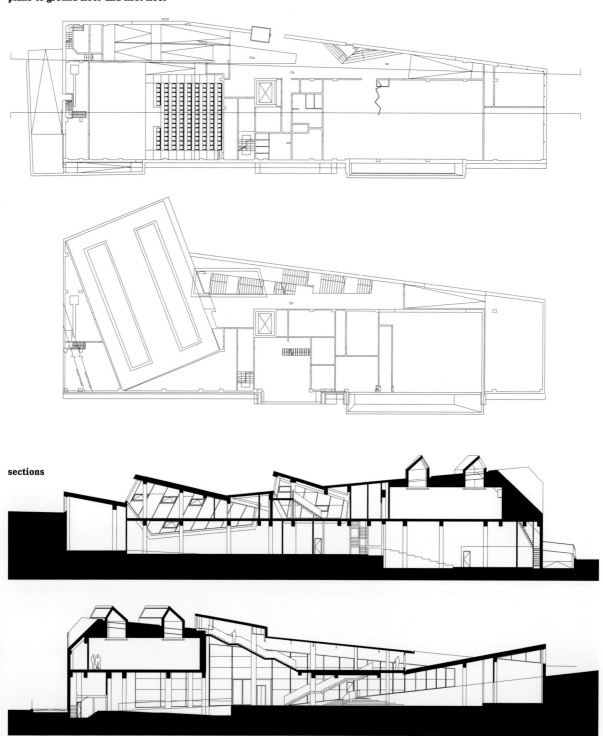

sections

Dennis Gilbert/VIEW

7 - 1974
Art Collection

Tuath na Mara

view from sea

Dennis Gilbert/VIEW

detail of elevation

Dennis Gilbert/VIEW

site plan

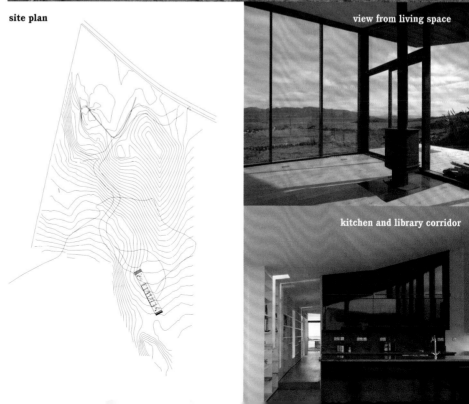

view from living space

kitchen and library corridor

Teach Annie

detail of elevation *Andy Frew*

plan of ground floor   plan of first floor

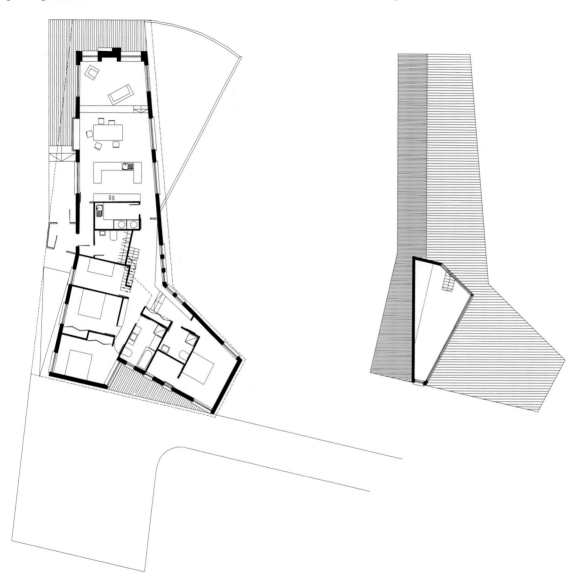

house in landscape

Dennis Gilbert/VIEW

living space

aerie

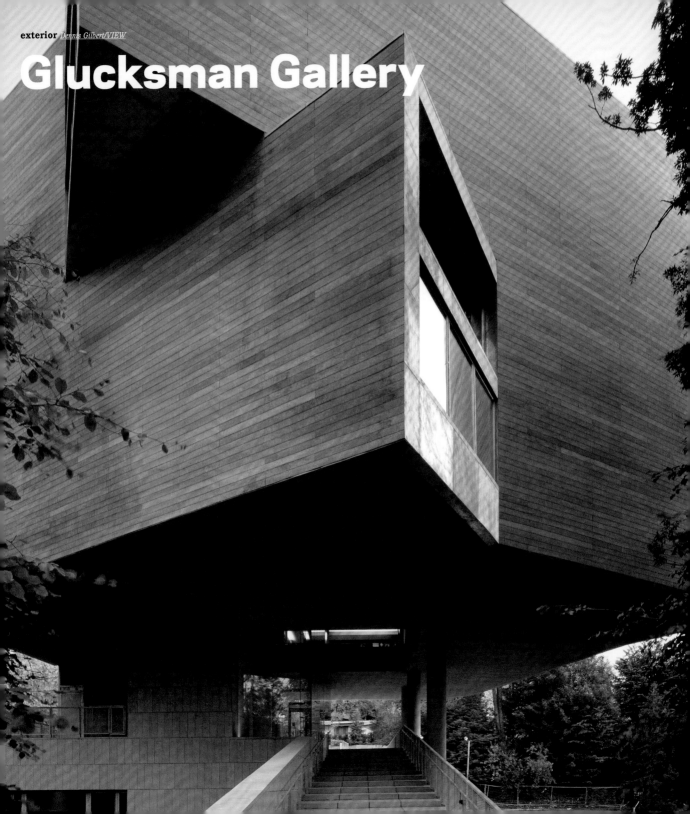

Glucksman Gallery

O'Donnell + Tuomey Architects

To write a new perspective on the work of O'Donnell + Tuomey is a considerable challenge. The firm not only attracts great attention and admiration from architects and critics who generate large volumes of attendant literature, but its principals also write a good deal themselves. Moreover, they have been at the forefront of architecture in Ireland for years. After working in London at Stirling Wilford on the Staatsgalerie in Stuttgart, Sheila O'Donnell and John Tuomey returned to Ireland and became key members of Group 91. Possibly Ireland's best-known practice outside the island, their firm has been short-listed twice for the Stirling Prize; as teachers, they have played a critical part in the education of at least one generation of Ireland's architects.

Though these are clearly two practitioners preoccupied by architecture, they are as likely to discuss poetry or recent travels with you as their latest building. They seem to teach, paint, design exhibitions, lecture, and create architecture as one move; none of these actions is without long consideration and immersion with the others. Each of their projects evolves from the previous. The firm uses this kind of careful, experienced growth to its advantage; other practices, less focused and intense, might not allow this kind of memory to develop and be utilized.

The importance of site runs through the body of their work from its earliest days to the larger commissions of recent times. For O'Donnell + Tuomey, a great building "becomes part of the identity of the place, as if it always belonged"; they seem to listen to the "murmur" of sites in the manner of Rafael Moneo. They maintain that an understanding of site can be accomplished whether the building is urban or rural. There are "geographical fault lines" on every site, and part of their work "distills the essence of the place to these natural or naturally scaled phenomena."

In recent years, the firm has worked on major civic projects with considerable symbolic importance. At the same time, "We're big fans of the ordinary, the elevated ordinary," O'Donnell asserts. Their architecture is willing to be quiet, to act as a backdrop for people's lives as housing and schools. They hope that, like the Georgian terraces of Dublin, their buildings provide proportion, excellent light, and useful repetition of elements that create good architecture. Rather than create architectural bombasts, they maintain that "the event is what happens in the building, not the building itself."

The Glucksman Gallery, one of the best-known Irish buildings in the last decade, highlights O'Donnell + Tuomey's commitment to creating buildings that not only respond to their place but make the site "more itself" with the insertion of their architecture. The original plan by University College Cork included a long, low building that stretched along the length of a partially wooded riverbank field. O'Donnell + Tuomey, though, knew that the right building for the place was one that would rear up on its back legs and enter the existing canopy. Tuomey explains that "the Glucksman reveals its own site and allows the site to realize itself, on the river, in the trees."

After entering through a stone plinth, anchored to the ground, the visitor is then taken up, turning, through the base of the building into the upper reaches of the galleries, three and four stories above the river and landscape below. As the building program changes, so do the materials—from limestone cladding to concrete to a sustainable hardwood timber, Angelim de Campagna. O'Donnell + Tuomey was not, thankfully, prepared to then foist a boring white cube of a galley onto the building; instead, the display spaces feature curved walls that respond to the external landscape and fenestration, to bring into the display space views of the leafy campus in the foreground and of the city of Cork beyond.

Killiney House, in the well-heeled suburbs south of Dublin, is a building that emerges from the sloped granite outcrop in which it sits. It is part house, part crag. Because the roof is the building's main facade, it feels as if the building has grown down from the roof; the granite ground plane melds into roof, and the building roots into the ground beneath. Like the Glucksman Gallery, the house turns on a subtle axis, with quieter bedrooms to the roadside of the site; the more public living spaces radiate toward the reason one builds a house in Killiney—the jaw-dropping view. This building makes use of multiple split-levels, revealing numerous choices throughout. It reminds one considerably of an Adolf Loos house with its many views, though O'Donnell + Tuomey's are more unruly, as befits the surroundings. Granite-clad concrete used in the house roots it to the site, but the angled planes of the ceilings and roofscape carry the inhabitant skyward. Indeed, one of the best spaces of the house is on the roof of the main bedroom. The concrete's rawness is tempered here through sandblasting that exposes mica in the aggregate, revealing what should be, but somehow isn't, incongruous delicacy. Killiney House is formally unlike other O'Donnell + Tuomey buildings—playing more freely in section, devising a radiating plan—but remains rooted in their sensitivity to site.

The Cherry Orchard School represents a renewed interest in Ireland's city councils in providing infrastructure not only for physical aspects such as traffic, water supply, and waste management but also for the community's lives and culture as well. This is the making not of buildings alone but of society, with, one might say, O'Donnell and Tuomey acting as critical theorists. The school houses children with special needs in its upper stories, and a primary school on the ground floor. The brief included spaces for children with serious problems at home. Babies are accommodated, too; as they age, they are introduced into play areas and even a

Dennis Gilbert/VIEW

plan of podium

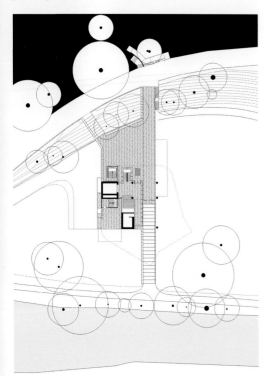

plan of second floor

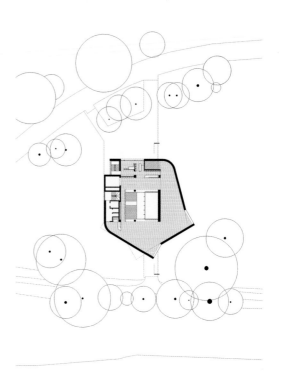

plan of top gallery

section

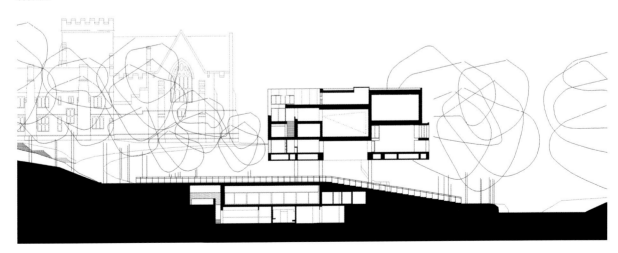

O'Donnell + Tuomey Architects **213**

"training" classroom, a slightly smaller scaled version of the space in which they will learn the following year. The building exudes O'Donnell + Tuomey's keen interest in architecture as backdrop for "events." The artwork of the school's children will form a palimpsest, like that of the architects' Integrated School at Ranelagh, that will become richer as students add layers to it.

The building is, for now, necessarily defensive, surrounded by high brick walls and screens of galvanized steel. Behind these walls, the building's brick combines with in-situ concrete vaults, specially commissioned artwork, and timber doors, windows, and panels. Throughout the day, light moves slowly through the building's pin-wheel plan, at times shaping the roof vault, at other times splaying window patterns of light and shadow on walls in the distance. In spring, the courtyards are filled with the white and pink blossoms of cherry trees planted into black asphalt playing areas in a grid. As they mature, these trees will give an indication on the other side of the wall of the activity—the "events" within.

The Sean O'Casey Community Centre takes many of its programmatic and material cues from the Cherry Orchard School. Like the school, the center is located in an area of Dublin that is undergoing redevelopment; similarly, the building provides a variety of facilities in four "blocks": crèche, large multipurpose rooms, theater, and interior gardens for recreation and reflection. The building, particularly on the ground floor, is inward turning. At Sean O'Casey, though, O'Donnell + Tuomey's tower includes meeting and work spaces with some of the best views over the city, providing a perspective of Dublin seldom seen or experienced in that area of the city. The building is located on the city's low-rise north side, near Dublin's docks, and as such feels disconnected from the rest of the urban area. The tower disabuses this lack of connection and, in addition, highlights the city's oft-ignored or unseen geography—the Dublin Mountains and

Irish Sea are visible beyond the human-made topography. Similarly, the tower, with its carefully corrugated concrete and Iroko-framed windows, reflects this neighborhood back to the rest of Dublin. The ground floor then allows for areas for more internalized activities, such as care of children or the elderly, dramatics (as befits a community center named for a renowned playwright), and sports. The entry foyer ties views and activity together in a broad, flowing space in which van Eyck–like moments—a bench, a shelf, a view into a courtyard—occur.

O'Donnell + Tuomey is one of the few firms from the Republic that works extensively in Northern Ireland. Among other projects, their Lyric Theatre is highly anticipated by both public and architects alike. One might expect the growing interest in Northern Ireland's architectural culture to be further advanced on completion of the building with a greater interest shown by clients for high-quality design, and by the "general public" for issues of the wider built environment.

gallery

entry

Killiney House

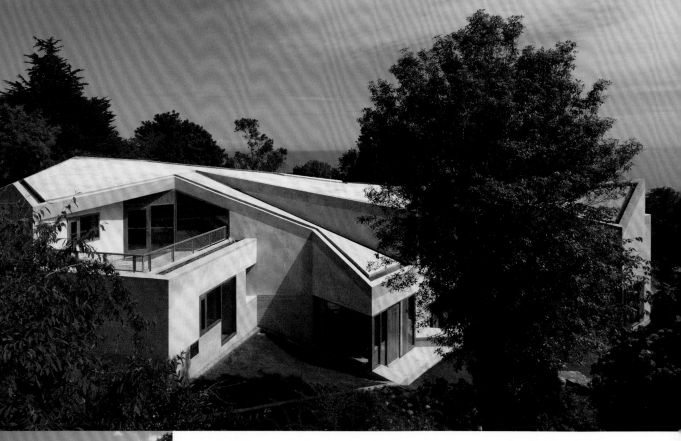

side elevation of entry

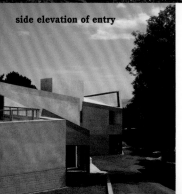

Dennis Gilbert/VIEW

view to Irish Sea

Dennis Gilbert/VIEW

detail of exterior

interior

plan of first floor

plan of second floor

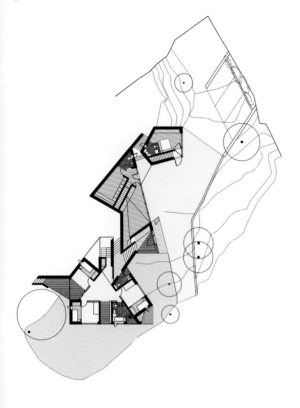

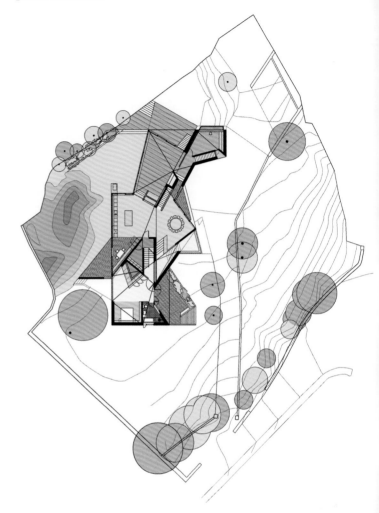

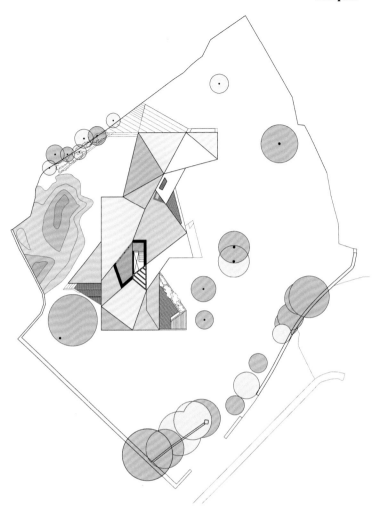

Cherry Orchard School

upper corridor

Dennis Gilbert/VIEW

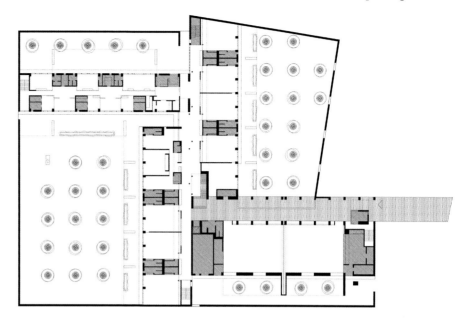

multipurpose hall *Dennis Gilbert/VIEW*

Sean O'Casey Community Centre

view from tower

Michael Moran

foyer

Michael Moran

tower from street

plan of ground floor

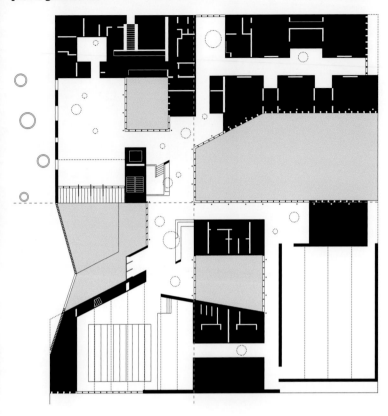

section

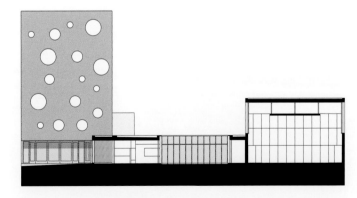

224 Full Irish

Knocktopher Friary

ODOS Architects

The youngest firm in this collection, ODOS, reflects a new trend: architects educated and trained in Ireland without the need to go abroad for long periods. Though David O'Shea worked in ABK London, he and partner Darrell O'Donoghue decided that the combination of building boom and the talent of architects at home were compelling reasons to stay in Dublin for their early professional experience.

As a practice, ODOS spent a significant period of their first few years knitting together old housing stock with crisp, light-filled extensions and freestanding buildings. The firm concentrates on the need to clean up sites, to regularize them, to sweep away the messy spatial accretions that invariably occur in urban domestic environments. ODOS has benefited from the leap of faith by clients, not only to trust a young firm questioning the essential nature of "what is a house" but also to provide a strongly contemporary answer to their problems. ODOS

aspires to create buildings that interrogate their sites, clients, and programmatic requirements alike while maintaining clarity in how the architecture is crafted. ODOS is committed to trying new materials with every project, drawing the experience into its quickly increasing palette.

The firm moved quickly from highly organized housing on cramped inner-city sites to the Knocktopher Friary, County Kilkenny. In contrast to earlier, tightly defined programs for housing, the Friary offered ODOS the opportunity to add a perambulation space to the interior side of a large courtyard as well as modest but sizeable bedrooms and an oratory for the community. In this project particularly, ODOS aspires to a reduction of materiality, avoiding the need to overly design elevations; glazing reaches floor to ceiling, and solid pieces reflect areas required on the interior for privacy. The firm's espousal of the notion of architectural "honesty" can be seen here, too;

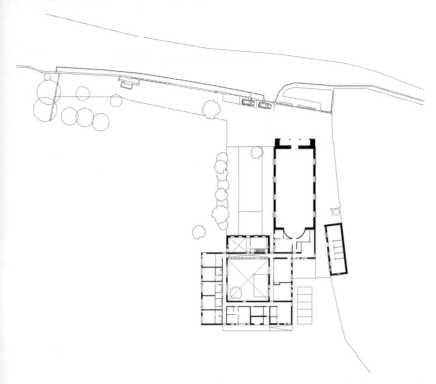

unadorned vertical timber contrasts with full-height glazing and with the boarded in-situ concrete in a subtle, simple pattern that carries over the continuous facade.

The House in Wicklow combines ODOS's previous inner-city experiences in organizing domestic space with the freer, more open site of the Friary. The house is sited beside a steep slope in a canted but essentially linear manner. The unremittingly modernist, hovering box, with its screening blue-gray panels to the road side, makes clear that this is a deliberate imposition in the landscape. This distinction between house and site, however, is mediated when one moves inside. The main living space is perched in an extremely deep overhang with large windows on its two opposite ends. This fenestration, along with large sliding glass door panels and glass balustrade to the deck, allows the site to visually run through the living space; the flow is made all the more dramatic by its elevation above the ground plane.

ODOS asserts that its considered, deliberate decisions present a "unique response to each condition." The architects admit that this constant need to consider every element of a project can become a poisoned chalice. It remains, though, a piece of silverware they would be loath to do without.

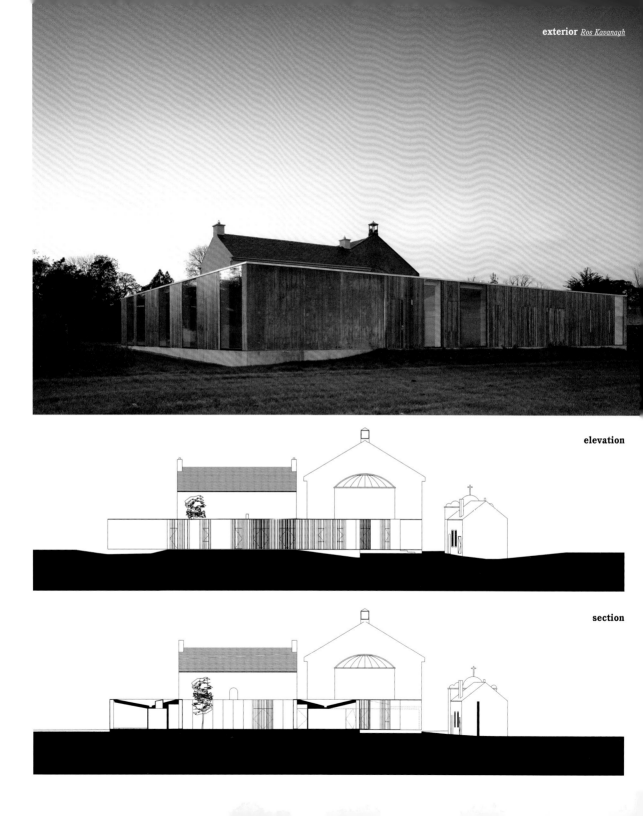

elevation

section

House in Wicklow

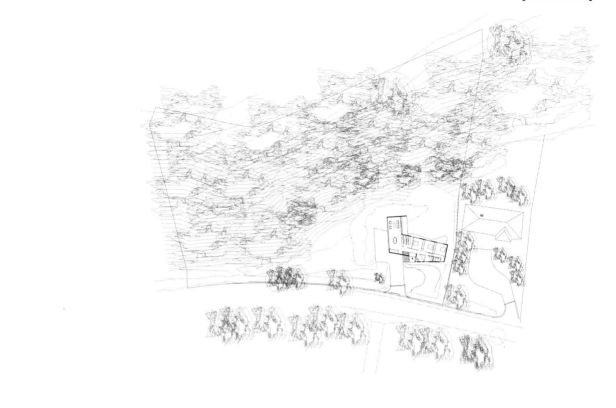

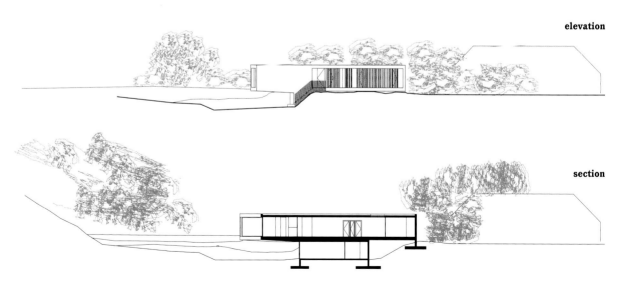

Ros Kavanagh

Acknowledgments

Inevitably, a book like this requires reams of thank-yous; just as inevitably, I will have forgotten someone. For that, I offer my most sincere apologies. Thanks to Kevin Lippert and Clare Jacobson for calling and asking if I wanted to write a book; thanks to patient Paul Harron and the generous Northern Ireland Arts Council for funding me to run around the country to look at gorgeous buildings and talk to interesting people; thanks to all the architects for their time, input, hard work, and talent; thanks to the photographers who made the book a lovely thing; thanks to Jan Haux for graphic skill and graphic patience; thanks to the clients with whom I spent valuable hours; thanks to the librarians at Queens University Science Library, who taught me about www.paddi.net, the database of Irish architecture, and ferreted out hundreds of files for me to study; thanks to Dick Combs for his help with funding applications; thanks to the governments of North and South, who have provided the beginnings of good public transportation links; thanks to Shane O'Toole and his frighteningly vast knowledge about the Venice Biennale and Irish architecture in general; thanks to Emmett Scanlon of the Arts Council for discussing the state of Irish architecture; thanks to the beloved and much-missed Eugene Santomasso for making writing about architecture fun in the first place; and thanks to mom and dad for liking Ireland as much as I do. Most of all, though, thanks to ARF, who kept me in Ireland and focused on the bigger things.